Structure & Speaking Practice
Seoul

NATIONAL GEOGRAPHIC
L E A R N I N G

Australia • Brazil • Mexico • Singapore • United Kingdom • United States

National Geographic Learning,
a Cengage Company

Structure & Speaking Practice, Seoul

Nancy Douglas and James R. Morgan

Publisher: Sherrise Roehr

Executive Editor: Laura LeDréan

Managing Editor: Jennifer Monaghan

Digital Implementation Manager,
Irene Boixareu

Senior Media Researcher: Leila Hishmeh

Director of Global Marketing: Ian Martin

Regional Sales and National Account
Manager: Andrew O'Shea

Content Project Manager: Ruth Moore

Senior Designer: Lisa Trager

Manufacturing Planner: Mary Beth
Hennebury

Composition: Lumina Datamatics

For permission to use material from this text or product,
submit all requests online at **cengage.com/permissions**
Further permissions questions can be emailed to
permissionrequest@cengage.com

Student Edition: Structure & Speaking Practice, Seoul
ISBN-13: 978-0-357-13791-8

National Geographic Learning
20 Channel Center Street
Boston, MA 02210
USA

Locate your local office at **international.cengage.com/region**

Visit National Geographic Learning online at **ELTNGL.com**
Visit our corporate website at **www.cengage.com**

Printed in China
Print Number: 01   Print Year: 2019

Photo Credits

SCOPE & SEQUENCE

Unit / Lesson	Video	Vocabulary	Listening

Grammar	Pronunciation	Speaking	Reading	Writing	Communication
Review of the simple present tense Describing appearance using *be / have*	Question intonation review	Introducing yourself; Asking about occupations	Celebrity doubles Skim for gist Scan for details	Describe a classmate	Ask questions to find classmates with various interests Describe a person
Review of the present continuous tense Subject and object pronouns	Listening for contractions	Greeting people and asking how they are	World greetings Preview the reading Make predictions Scan for details Read for details	Write a text message	Draw a place your partner describes Act out and guess actions
The simple past tense with *be* The simple past: affirmative and negative statements	Past tense -*ed* endings	Agreeing or disagreeing with an opinion	Eco-fuel Africa Make predictions Infer information Sequence events Read for details	Write about a personal hero	Plan a party and invite famous people Discuss who should be given an award for being a hero
The present continuous as future -*ed* / -*ing* adjectives	Syllable stress	Taking and leaving a message	A movie remake Use background knowledge Make predictions Check predictions Read for details	Write about a movie you like	Create a new movie and make a poster Talk about favorite movies

Language Summaries p. 66   Grammar Notes p. 70

PEOPLE

Look at the photo. Answer the questions.

1 What kinds of people do you see?

2 What are the people doing?

3 What are they thinking about?

UNIT GOALS

1 Ask questions to get basic personal information

2 Introduce yourself

3 Talk about where you come from and what you do

4 Describe a person's appearance

People look at an art exhibition in Santiago de Compostela, Spain.

LESSON A GETTING TO KNOW YOU

People on a busy street in New York City

1 VIDEO World's Biggest Melting Pot

A Look at the photo of New York City. What do you notice about it? Tell a partner.

B Watch the video. Circle your answers.
1. Welcome to Brooklyn / Queens New York.
2. Almost half the people here were born in New York / another country.
3. They speak almost 50 / 150 languages.

half = 50%

C Watch the video again. Complete the sentences.
1. "I'm from Madras, the southern part of India. My _____ live there and my grandparents live there."
2. "My mom's from South Korea and on my father's side I am _____, Irish, English..."
3. "So you have Eastern Europeans. You have Hispanics. You have _____. You have Arabic. I like that."

D Is your city similar to or different from this neighborhood? Use your answers in **B** and **C** to explain to a partner.

2 VOCABULARY

A Look at Silvia's LinkBook page. Do you have a page like this?

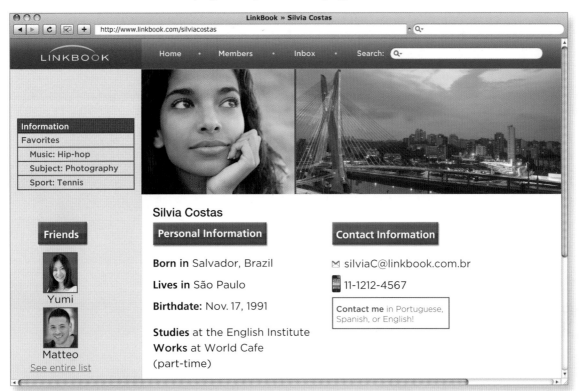

LinkBook » Silvia Costas

http://www.linkbook.com/silviacostas

LINKBOOK   Home   •   Members   •   Inbox   •   Search: Q▾

Information
Favorites
Music: Hip-hop
Subject: Photography
Sport: Tennis

Friends

Yumi

Matteo
See entire list

Silvia Costas

Personal Information

Born in Salvador, Brazil

Lives in São Paulo

Birthdate: Nov. 17, 1991

Studies at the English Institute
Works at World Cafe
(part-time)

Contact Information

✉ silviaC@linkbook.com.br

📱 11-1212-4567

Contact me in Portuguese,
Spanish, or English!

ℹ **Saying email addresses**

silviaC@linkbook
.com.br = silvia C
(at) linkbook (dot)
com (dot) b-r

B Look at Silvia's web page. Complete the questions and answers with a partner. Use the words in the box.

born	city	first name	hometown	job	last name
phone	email address	friends	interested in	languages	subject

1. What's your _____?   (It's) Silvia.
2. What's your _____?   (It's) Costas.
3. Where were you born?   I was _____ in Salvador. It's my _____.
4. Where do you live now?   São Paulo. It's a fun _____!
5. What do you do for fun?   I'm in a band with my _____, Yumi and Matteo.
6. What's your favorite _____?   I'm _____ photography.
7. How many _____ do you speak?   Three. I speak Portuguese, Spanish, and English.
8. What's your _____?   (It's) silviaC@linkbook.com.br.
9. What's your _____ number?   (It's) 11-1212-4567.
10. What do you do?   I'm a student, and I have a part-time _____.

C Use the questions in **B** to interview your partner.

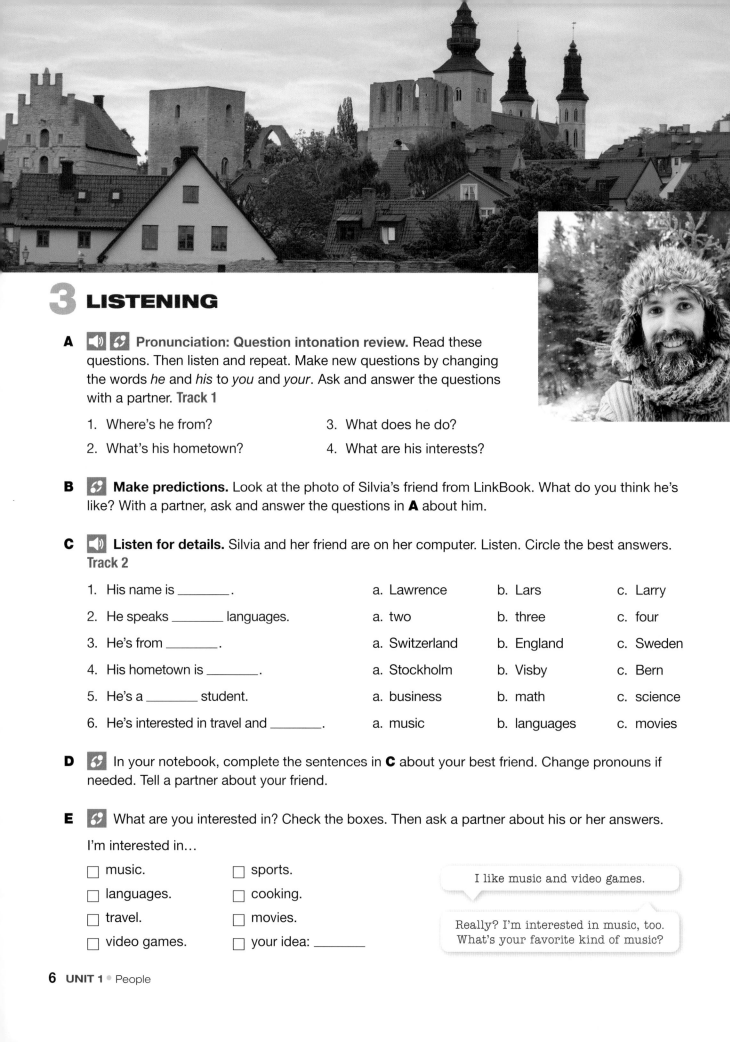

3 LISTENING

A 🔊 🔁 **Pronunciation: Question intonation review.** Read these questions. Then listen and repeat. Make new questions by changing the words *he* and *his* to *you* and *your*. Ask and answer the questions with a partner. **Track 1**

1. Where's he from?
2. What's his hometown?
3. What does he do?
4. What are his interests?

B 🔁 **Make predictions.** Look at the photo of Silvia's friend from LinkBook. What do you think he's like? With a partner, ask and answer the questions in **A** about him.

C 🔊 **Listen for details.** Silvia and her friend are on her computer. Listen. Circle the best answers. **Track 2**

1. His name is _____.	a. Lawrence	b. Lars	c. Larry
2. He speaks _____ languages.	a. two	b. three	c. four
3. He's from _____.	a. Switzerland	b. England	c. Sweden
4. His hometown is _____.	a. Stockholm	b. Visby	c. Bern
5. He's a _____ student.	a. business	b. math	c. science
6. He's interested in travel and _____.	a. music	b. languages	c. movies

D 🔁 In your notebook, complete the sentences in **C** about your best friend. Change pronouns if needed. Tell a partner about your friend.

E 🔁 What are you interested in? Check the boxes. Then ask a partner about his or her answers.

I'm interested in…

☐ music.
☐ languages.
☐ travel.
☐ video games.

☐ sports.
☐ cooking.
☐ movies.
☐ your idea: _____

> I like music and video games.

> Really? I'm interested in music, too. What's your favorite kind of music?

4 SPEAKING

A 🔊 Mariana and Danny live in the same apartment building. Listen. Are they meeting for the first time? How do you know? **Track 3**

MARIANA: Hi. My name is Mariana. I'm in apartment 201.

DANNY: Hi, Mariana. I'm Danny. I'm in 302. It's nice to meet you.

MARIANA: Nice to meet you, too.

DANNY: So, are you a student, Mariana?

MARIANA: Yeah, I study music at NYU.

DANNY: That's interesting.

MARIANA: What do you do, Danny?

DANNY: I'm a student at Hunter College. I also work in an art gallery.

B 🔄 Practice the conversation with a partner. Then practice with *your* information.

SPEAKING STRATEGY

C 👥 Introduce yourself to four classmates. Then ask about their names and occupations. Complete the chart with their information. Use the Useful Expressions to help you.

Useful Expressions	
Introducing yourself	**Asking about occupations**
A: My name is Mariana.	A: What do you do?
B: Hi, I'm Danny. (It's) Nice to meet you.	B: I'm a music student.
A: (It's) Nice to meet you, too.	
Speaking tip	
When you are introducing yourself, *My name is...* and *I'm...* can both be used.	

Name	Occupation
Clara	student (studies art)
1.	
2.	
3.	
4.	

D 🔄 Tell a partner about the classmates you talked to in **C**.

> Clara is a student. She studies art.

5 GRAMMAR

A Turn to page 70. Complete the exercise. Then do **B–E** below.

Review of the Simple Present Tense		
	Questions	**Answers**
Yes / No questions with be	**Are** you a student? **Is** he a student?	Yes, I **am**. / No, I'm not. Yes, he **is**. / No, he's not.
Yes / No questions with other verbs	**Do** you **speak** English? **Does** she **speak** English?	Yes, I **do**. / No, I **don't**. Yes, she **does**. / No, she **doesn't**.
Wh- questions	What do you do? What does she do?	I'm a student. She's a doctor.

B Steffi is writing about herself and her classmate. Read the sentences. Write the correct form of each verb.

Monika and Me

Monika (1. be) ___is___ my classmate. We (2. be) _____ different in many ways. I (3. be) _____ an only child. Monika (4. have) _____ two brothers and a sister. I (5. live) _____ with my family. Monika (6. live) _____ in her own apartment. We both go to Western University, but I (7. study) _____ English literature and Monika (8. study) _____ business. I (9. not have) _____ a job, but Monika (10. work) _____ part-time in a cafe. I (11. love) _____ dance music, but Monika (12. not like) _____ it. She (13. listen) _____ to rap. Monika and I (14. watch) _____ TV together on the weekends.

C 🔁 Complete questions 1–4 with the correct form of *be* or *do*. Complete questions 5–8 with a *Wh-* question word. Take turns asking and answering the questions with a partner.

1. _____ Steffi and Monika different?

2. _____ Steffi an only child?

3. _____ Steffi study business?

4. _____ Monika and Steffi go to the same university?

5. _____ subject does Steffi study?

6. _____ does Monika work?

7. _____ does Steffi live with?

8. _____ does Monika live?

D Complete each sentence with an affirmative or negative verb in the box to make it true for you.

speak	have	study	like

1. I _____ a middle name.

2. I _____ my first name.

3. I _____ more than one language well.

4. I _____ on the weekend.

5. I _____ my hometown.

6. I _____ a favorite subject at school.

E 🔁 How are you and your partner similar and different? Use the sentences in **D** to form questions. Ask follow-up questions.

> Do you have a middle name?   Yes, I do.   What is it?   It's Victor.

6 COMMUNICATION

A 👥 For each item in the chart, ask the question until you find a person who answers *Yes*. Write his or her name. Then ask one follow-up question and write the extra information.

ℹ️ Follow-up questions are an important part of conversation. Make sure to ask a follow-up question related to what your partner already said. *Wh-* questions usually work better than *Yes / No* questions.

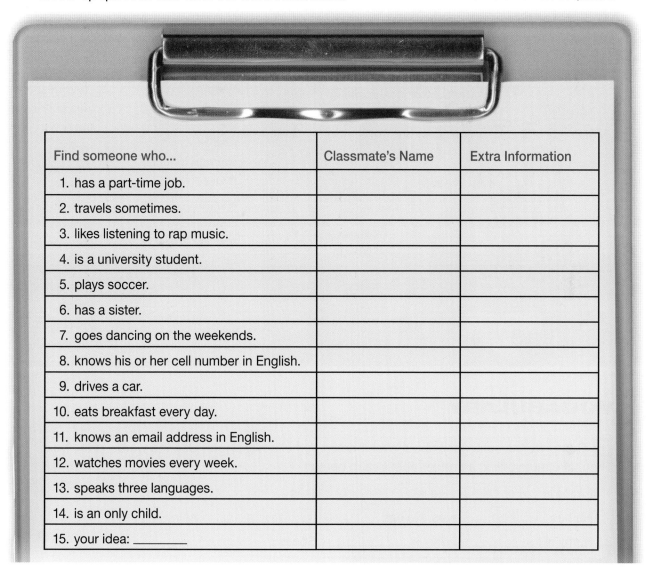

Find someone who...	Classmate's Name	Extra Information
1. has a part-time job.		
2. travels sometimes.		
3. likes listening to rap music.		
4. is a university student.		
5. plays soccer.		
6. has a sister.		
7. goes dancing on the weekends.		
8. knows his or her cell number in English.		
9. drives a car.		
10. eats breakfast every day.		
11. knows an email address in English.		
12. watches movies every week.		
13. speaks three languages.		
14. is an only child.		
15. your idea: _____		

> Do you have a part-time job?
>
> Yes, I do.

> What do you do?
>
> I work in a bookstore.

B 🔄 Tell a classmate about the people in your chart.

Michael, 19

Emilio, 52

Alexis, 23 Ashley, 23

Kathy, 48

Use *be* with...	Use *have* with...
Age	**Eye color**
young	(dark) brown
in his / her teens*	blue
in his / her twenties*	green
elderly (80+)	**Hairstyle**
Weight	long ↔ short
skinny	straight ↔ curly
thin	wavy
slim**	spiky
average weight	**Hair color**
heavy	black
Height	(light / dark) brown
short	blond
average height	red
tall	gray
	Facial hair
	beard
	mustache

*teens (13–19), twenties (ages 20–29), thirties, forties

**Slim* means skinny / thin, but *slim* has a positive meaning.

1 VOCABULARY

A Complete the sentences about each person in the family photo. Use the words in the box. Then take turns telling a partner about each person.

1. Emilio is ___in his fifties___ . He is ___tall___ . He is ___average weight___ .
   <small>age   height   weight</small>
   He has ___brown___ eyes. He has ___short___ , ___gray___ hair.

2. Kathy is _____ . She is _____ . She is _____ .
   <small>age   height   weight</small>
   She has _____ eyes. She has _____ , straight, _____ hair.

3. Michael is _____ . He is _____ . He is _____ .
   <small>age   height   weight</small>
   He has _____ eyes. He has _____ , _____ , _____ hair.

4. Alexis and Ashley are _____ . They are _____ . They are _____ .
   <small>age   height   weight</small>
   They have _____ eyes. They have _____ , wavy hair.

B Answer the questions with a partner.

1. Who does Michael look like? He **looks like** ___his father___ . They're both tall.
2. Who does Ashley look like? She **looks like** _____ . They both have red hair.
3. Who do you look like? I **look like** _____ . We're both... / We both have...

> I look like my mom. We're both tall and slim, and we both have dark, curly hair.

2 LISTENING

A ⟳ **Use background knowledge.** Look at the pictures below. Describe the man's appearance in each one. Tell a partner.

a. ☐    b. ☐    c. ☐

B 🔊 **Listen for gist.** Read the sentence below. Then listen and complete it.

Emily is at the airport. She is ___ her uncle Tim. **Track 4**

a. traveling with   b. looking for   c. talking to   d. shopping for

C 🔊 **Listen for details.** Now listen to the entire conversation. Circle the words that describe Uncle Tim before and now. Then check (✓) the correct picture of Uncle Tim <u>now</u> in **A**. **Track 5**

1. Uncle Tim <u>before</u>:

   short / tall   short hair / long hair   brown hair / blond hair

2. Uncle Tim <u>now</u>:

   short / tall   short hair / long hair   brown hair / blond hair

D ⟳ Think about your appearance in the past. Is anything different now? Complete the sentences. Tell a partner.

In the past, I was _____.

Now I am _____.

In the past, I had _____.

Now I have _____.

> In the past, I had short, brown hair. Now I have long, blond hair.

3 READING 🔊 Track 6

A 🔁 Look at the photo. Who are these people? What do they do? Tell a partner.

B **Skim for gist.** Read the passage. Then complete the sentence below.

The reading is mainly about _____.

a. the actor Daniel Radcliffe

b. people who look like celebrities

c. good-looking actors

d. famous people with a lot of money

C **Scan for details.** Quickly find and underline the answers to questions 1 and 2 in the reading.

1. How does Andrew Walker make money?

2. How do celebrity doubles make money?

D 🔁 Answer the questions with a partner.

1. Look at the photo of the two men singing. Do they look alike? Why or why not?

2. Is being a celebrity double fun? Why or why not?

3. Do you (or someone you know) look like a famous person? Who? Explain.

CELEBRITY DOUBLES

A group of teenagers is standing outside a shop in Manchester, England. Many of them have cameras and are looking in the shop window. They want to see celebrity Daniel Radcliffe. A man in the shop looks like Radcliffe. He has brown hair and Radcliffe's good looks. But the young man in the shop isn't the famous actor. He's Andrew Walker, a 22-year-old shop clerk.

Actor Daniel Radcliffe

Walker isn't surprised by the teenagers. People often stop him on the street and want to take his picture. Walker is a clerk, but he also makes money as Radcliffe's double. Walker travels all over Europe as Daniel Radcliffe. It's an exciting life for the shop clerk from Manchester.

Today, many companies work with celebrity doubles. The most popular celebrity doubles look like famous athletes, pop singers, and actors. The companies pay doubles to go to parties and business meetings. Doubles are also on TV and in commercials.

Some celebrities even dress up as doubles. American talk show host Jimmy Fallon is famous for dressing up and performing as famous musicians. He looks and sounds just like them. Sometimes the real musicians even come on his show!

4 GRAMMAR

A Turn to page 71. Complete the exercises. Then do **B–D** below.

	Describing Appearance		
Subject	***be / have***	**Adjective**	**Noun**
He	**is**	tall.	
		average	height / weight.
		young / in his teens.	
	has	blue	eyes.
		spiky, black	hair.

B Work with a partner. Practice the conversation. Can you guess the person? Check your answer on the bottom of the page.

A: I'm thinking of a famous person.

B: Is it a woman?

A: No, it's a man.

B: Is he British?

A: No, he's not. He's from Argentina.

B: Is he tall?

A: No, he's not. He's a little short.

B: Is he in his twenties?

A: Yes, I think he's in his late twenties.

B: Does he have long hair?

A: No, he doesn't.

B: Is he a soccer player?

A: Yes, he is.

B: I know! It's…

C Think of a famous person. Complete the notes below.

Name: _____   Hair: _____   Height: _____

Job: _____   Eyes: _____   Weight: _____

Nationality: _____   Age: _____

D Ask your partner seven questions. Try to guess his or her person. Then switch roles.

5 WRITING

A Read the paragraph on the right. Then write five or six sentences about a classmate's appearance on a separate piece of paper. Use the paragraph as a model. Don't write your classmate's name.

B Exchange papers with a partner.

1. Are there any mistakes in your partner's writing? If yes, circle them.

2. Can you guess the person? Write his or her name on the paper.

> My classmate is in his twenties. He's average height—he's about 172 centimeters. He has short, straight, brown hair. He has dark brown eyes (I think). He doesn't wear glasses.

Answer B: Lionel Messi

6 COMMUNICATION

A Work in a group of four. Each person chooses a photo above. Think about your answers to the questions below.

1. What does the person in your photo look like? Describe him or her.

2. In your opinion, is the person good-looking? Why or why not?

B Tell the group your answers in **A**. Do your partners agree with you? Why or why not?

> I think he's very handsome.

> He's OK. I don't like his beard or hairstyle.

C Now find a photo of someone else online. Show it to your group. Then repeat **A** and **B**.

Word Bank
Other words to describe appearance
Has...
a nice smile
a tattoo
Is...
pretty
handsome
good-looking

2 BEHAVIOR

Look at the photo. Answer the questions.

1 What are these people doing?

2 How do they feel?

3 Why do you think they feel that way?

UNIT GOALS

1 Talk about actions happening now

2 Greet other people and ask how they are

3 Describe how you feel

4 Talk about and use common gestures

A tango performance in Buenos Aires, Argentina

1 VIDEO Can You Spot a Fake Smile?

A Look at this photo. Are the smiles genuine or not? Why do you think so? Tell a partner.

B Watch the video. You are going to see three pairs of photos. Choose the person with the <u>fake</u> smile in each pair.

1. LEFT   RIGHT
2. LEFT   RIGHT
3. LEFT   RIGHT

C Could you spot the fake smiles? Compare your score with a partner's score.

D Watch again. Circle the correct answer. Do you agree with the answer?

To spot a fake smile, look at the person's eyes / face / mouth.

2 VOCABULARY

A Work with a partner. Read these sentences. Who is doing what? Match the sentences to the people in the picture. Write the correct letter. Not all letters will be used.

1. She's **smiling** at her friend. _b_

2. She's **pointing** at the man. ____

3. He's **shouting** at the woman. ____

4. She's **waving** goodbye to her daughter. ____

5. She's **talking** to her friend. ____

6. It's **barking** at the girl. ____

7. He's **looking** outside. ____

8. She's **sitting** on the bench. ____

9. She's **walking** down the street. ____

10. She's **running**. ____

B Now cover up the sentences in **A**. Work with a partner. Take turns describing the picture. Try to talk about all of the people.

> Let's see... two women are talking and walking together. I think they are friends....

3 LISTENING

A 🔊 **Pronunciation: Listening for contractions.** Read the sentences. Then listen and repeat. Notice the difference between the sentences in each pair. **Track 7**

1a. I am talking to you!

1b. I'm talking to you!

2a. Oh yes, it is mine. Thanks!

2b. Oh yes, it's mine. Thanks!

3a. We are too busy today.

3b. We're too busy today.

4a. How is it going?

4b. How's it going?

B 🔊 **Pronunciation: Listening for contractions.** Now listen to four short dialogs. For each one, circle the sentence in **A** that you hear. **Track 8**

C 🔊 **Distinguish speakers.** Look at the picture on page 19 as you listen to these five conversations. Write the letters of the people from the picture speaking in each one. **Track 9**

Conversation 1: ___d___

Conversation 2: _____ _____

Conversation 3: _____ _____

Conversation 4: _____ _____

Conversation 5: _____ _____

D 🔊 **Infer information.** Listen again. Match each situation with the appropriate verb. One verb is extra. **Track 9**

asking	looking	saying
helping	meeting	shouting

1. The woman is _____ goodbye to her daughter.

2. The woman is _____ the man.

3. The man is _____ at the woman.

4. The girl is _____ her mother something.

5. The two friends are _____.

E 🔊 👥 Listen to Conversation 5 again. With a partner, write an ending to it. Then role-play your conversation for another pair. **Track 10**

4 SPEAKING

A 🔊 🔁 Read the conversation and listen. Why is Katy worried? What is Jim's idea? Tell a partner. **Track 11**

JIM: Hi, Katy.

KATY: Hey, Jim. How's it going?

JIM: Great! How are you doing?

KATY: So-so.

JIM: Yeah? What's wrong?

KATY: Oh, I have an important test tomorrow.

JIM: But you're not studying.

KATY: Well, I'm kind of tired.

JIM: Why don't you take a break and drink some coffee? We can go to a cafe together.

KATY: And then I can study later. Sounds good!

B 🔁 Practice the conversation with a partner. Then ask your partner how he or she is today.

SPEAKING STRATEGY

C 🔁 Read the two situations below. With a partner, write two new conversations on a sheet of paper. Use the conversation in **A** and the Useful Expressions to help you.

Situation 1

Student A: You're worried. You have two tickets to a basketball game tonight. You're going with your friend, but your friend is late.

Student B: Your suggestion: Take a taxi to the game. Maybe the friend is there.

Situation 2

Student A: You're unhappy. You live in Toronto. Your cousin lives in Boston. She wants you to visit her. Plane tickets are expensive right now.

Student B: Your suggestion: Rent a car and drive from Toronto to Boston.

Useful Expressions
Greeting people and asking how they are
☺ A: Hi, _____. How's it going?
B: Fine. / OK. / All right. / Pretty good. / Not bad. How about you?
A: I'm fine.
☹ A: Hi, _____. How are you doing?
B: So-so. / Not so good.
A: Really? What's wrong?
B: I'm (a little) worried. / I'm (kind of) tired. I have a big test tomorrow.

Word Bank
kind of = a little

D 👥 Role-play one conversation for another pair.

5 GRAMMAR

A Turn to page 72. Complete the exercise. Then do **B** and **C** below.

Review of the Present Continuous Tense			
Affirmative and negative statements			
I'm / She's / They're	(not)	going	to the party.

Wh- and Yes / No questions					**Answers**
	Are	you	going	to the party?	Yes, I am. / No, I'm not.
When	are				In about an hour.

Use the present continuous for actions happening now: subject + *am* / *is* / *are* + verb *-ing*

B Ask and answer questions about the people in the picture.

1a. Where are they _____? On the sofa.

1b. What are they _____? Coffee.

2. _____ they talking? No, they're _____.

3. _____ she opening a present? Yes, she _____.

4. _____ he enjoying the music? No, he _____.

C Take turns acting out one of the actions below for your partner. You can also add your own ideas to the list.

driving a car / riding a bicycle / riding a horse

waking up late / taking a shower / brushing your teeth

eating noodles / eating an ice cream cone / eating steak

drinking coffee / drinking juice / drinking soda

putting on a pair of jeans / putting on a winter coat / putting on a pair of boots

your own ideas: _____

> Let's see... you're drinking something. I know, it's juice! No? OK then, maybe you're drinking...

6 COMMUNICATION

A Think of a place in your city or a famous place in the world. Write it down. (Don't show anyone!)

_____

B Imagine you are in the place you wrote down in **A**. What do you see? What are people doing? Write four or five sentences about your place. See the example for ideas.

Example: It's a beautiful city. There is a lot of water. Some people are riding in a boat. A man is standing in the boat. He is pushing. They are going under a bridge.

_____

_____

_____

_____

_____

_____

Venice, Italy

C Do the following:

Student A: Read your sentences from **B** to a partner.

Student B: Draw the place your partner describes in the box below.

Student A: Check your partner's drawing. Is it accurate? Can your partner guess the place?

D Switch roles and do **C** again.

confident

relaxed

embarrassed	~~relaxed~~	excited	bored	confused
nervous / worried	sad	happy	angry	~~confident~~

1 VOCABULARY

A 🔄 Look at the photos. How do the people feel? Point to a photo and tell a partner. Then write the correct word under each photo.

> She's angry.

B 🔄 Work with a partner.

1. **Student A:** Choose one feeling and act it out for your partner.
   Student B: Close your book. Guess your partner's feeling.

2. Change roles and repeat step 1. Do this until you act out all the feelings.

C 🔄 Ask and answer the questions below with a partner. Use a word from **A**. Explain your answers.

How do you feel...

- when you're waiting for the bus?
- before a big exam?
- when you speak English?

- about summer vacation?
- when a friend is always late?
- right now?

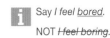 Say *I feel* <u>*bored*</u>.
NOT *I feel boring*.

2 LISTENING

A 🔊 **Understand a speaker's attitude.** Read sentences 1a–4a. Then listen. Circle the correct answer. **Track 12**

How do they feel?	Why?
1a. The man is excited about / bored with school.	1b. He wants to _____ his major.
2a. The woman is worried / confident about her exams.	2b. She _____ the information.
3a. The man is confident / confused about the address of the theater.	3b. The map on his phone is _____.
4a. The woman's boss is worried / angry. The woman is embarrassed / excited.	4b. The woman is _____ for work.

B 🔊 **Listen for details.** Listen again. Complete sentences 1b–4b with one word. **Track 12**

C 🔄 Look at the gestures. Complete each sentence with an expression from the box. Check your answers with a partner.

| Come here | Good luck | I don't know | Look (at that) |

1. You can shrug to say "_____."

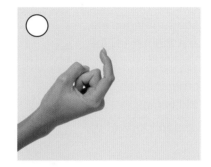

2. You can say "_____," by using your finger to call someone.

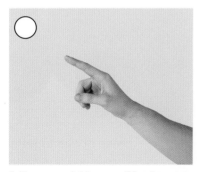

3. You can point to something to say "_____."

4. You can cross your fingers to say "_____."

D 🔊 **Infer information.** Listen again. Which gesture in **C** could be used in each conversation? Write the number of the conversation (1–4) on each photo. **Track 12**

E 🔄 Do the gestures in the photos have the same meaning in your country? Tell a partner.

3 READING 🔊 Track 13

A 🔄 **Preview the reading.** Look at the title and photos. Complete the definition and answer the question with a partner.

A *greeting* is a way to say _____.

What are the people in the photos doing?

B **Make predictions; Scan for details.** Guess where people use the greetings below: Brazil, New Zealand, or Japan? Write the country or countries. Then scan the reading to check your ideas.

Greeting	Country
1. bow	_____
2. kiss	_____
3. press noses	_____
4. shake hands	_____
5. wave	_____

C 🔄 **Read for details.** These sentences are false. Read the article. Make them true. Tell a partner.

1. In Brazil, women kiss other women as a greeting. Women don't kiss men.
2. When you shake hands, don't look at the person.
3. The Maori are the native people of Brazil.
4. In Japan, a smile always means you are happy.

D 🔄 In each situation below, what greeting do you use? What do you say? Tell a partner.

1. You see a friend in a cafe.
2. You interview for a job with Mr. Jones.
3. You meet your teacher on the street.
4. You see your boyfriend or girlfriend.

WORLD GREETINGS

press noses together

Brazil

Men often shake hands when they meet for the first time. When women meet, they touch cheeks and kiss. Women also kiss male friends to say hello.

Note: When you shake hands, look at the person. It's polite.[1]

kiss

New Zealand

In formal situations, both men and women usually shake hands when they meet someone for the first time. In informal situations, people often give a short wave and say "Hi."

Note: If you see two people pressing their noses together, they are probably Maori. The Maori are the native people of New Zealand. This is their traditional greeting.

shake hands

Japan

When people meet for the first time, they usually bow. In business, people also shake hands. In formal situations, people often exchange business cards. When you give a business card, it's polite to give it with two hands.

Note: In Japan, a smile can have different meanings. It usually means that the person is happy or that the person thinks something is funny. But it can also mean that the person is embarrassed.

bow

[1]If you are *polite*, you act in a respectful way.

4 GRAMMAR

A Turn to page 73. Complete the exercises. Then do **B–D** below.

Subject Pronouns	Object Pronouns
<u>I</u> love my parents.	My parents love **me**.
<u>You</u> need help.	I can help **you**.*
<u>He</u> / <u>She</u> knows Jon.	Jon knows **him** / **her**.
<u>It</u> is expensive.	I can't buy **it**.
<u>We</u> are having a party.	Please join **us**.
<u>They</u> are popular.	Everyone likes **them**.

*For both singular and plural *you*

> **i** **Object pronouns** come after...
> a verb: My parents *love* **me**.
> a preposition: Jon is angry *at* **her**.

B Complete the sentences with the correct object pronoun(s).

1. I speak English at school. Sometimes, I use _____ at home, too.

2. I have to take the university entrance exam soon. I'm worried about _____.

3. My cell phone is cool. My parents gave _____ to _____.

4. When I watch movies in English, I get confused. People talk fast. I can't understand _____.

5. Do you understand this grammar point? I can explain _____ to _____.

6. We are studying English. It can help _____ get jobs in the future.

7. _____ is my best friend. I talk to _____ every day.

C 🤝 Work with a partner. Check your answers in **B**. Which sentences are true for you? Which aren't? Why?

D 🤝 Which sentences in **B** aren't true for you? Change them so they are true and tell them to your partner.

5 WRITING

A 🤝 Koji and Paloma are classmates. They're texting. Match the underlined expressions with their meanings below. Then tell a partner: How does Paloma feel?

1. Are you _____

2. face-to-face _____

3. How are you? _____

4. OK _____

5. See you later. _____

6. Thanks. _____

B With your partner, complete the rules for texting. Can you think of other rules?

In texts, it's OK…	In informal situations (with friends)	In formal situations (with a teacher or boss)
1. not to capitalize words.	☑	☐
2. not to use punctuation.	☐	☐
3. to use abbreviations.	☐	☐
4. to use emoticons (smiley faces).	☐	☐

C In your notebook, rewrite the text conversation in **A** in full sentences. Add any missing words. Use correct punctuation and capitalization. Compare answers with a partner.

D Write a text to a partner in English. Use the expressions and emoticons in **A**. Do the following:

Student A: Imagine you have a school project to do. How do you feel? Text your partner.

Student B: Reply to your partner's text. Suggest working on the project together.

Student A: Agree and suggest a time to meet.

Student B: Reply to your partner's text.

Student A: Say "bye."

Student B: Say "bye."

E Read your partner's text and correct any mistakes. Then write a short reply to your partner to reschedule the meeting time.

6 COMMUNICATION

A Get into a group of three people. Read the directions to play this game.

Student A: Choose a sentence below. Act out the sentence for Students B and C. Do *not* use words.

Students B and C: Watch Student A. Be the first to say the sentence Student A is acting out. If you guess correctly, you get a point.

Take turns acting out the sentences. Play until all sentences are done.

I'm hungry.	Good luck!	He's crazy.
This is delicious.	Go away!	I'm nervous.
Stop it!	Look at that!	This tastes terrible.
Let's go!	Come here!	I'm not listening!
Be quiet.	I'm bored.	Sit down.
I'm sad.	I'm angry.	See you later.
Relax!	What? I can't hear you.	I'm not sure.

I know! You're saying "Come here!"

3 HEROES

Journalists and photographers travel to dangerous areas to share important stories with the world.

Alex Zanardi competes in a handcycle race.

1 VIDEO Touch the Sky

A Review the meaning of the words in the box with your instructor. Then look at the photo and read about Alex Zanardi. Try to complete the sentences with the words in the box. Two words are extra.

present		past
is	→	was
lose	→	lost
race	→	raced

arms	bikes	cars	legs

Alex Zanardi is a Formula 1 race car driver from Italy. In the past, he raced cars. Then he was in an accident. He lost his _____. Now he races _____.

B ▶ Watch the video. Check your answers in **A**.

C ▶ Watch again. Complete the quotes from Alex Zanardi.
1. (0:27): "Even the greatest d_____ can be turned into your greatest v_____."
2. (2:51): "I'm a l_____ person because at the age of 47, things are not over yet."

D 🔁 Answer the questions with a partner.
1. Look again at sentences 1 and 2 in **C**. What do they mean? Explain in your own words.
2. Do you agree with sentence 1?

Will Steger with his sled dogs

2 VOCABULARY

A Look at the photo and caption. Who is this person? What is he doing? Tell a partner.

B Read about Will Steger. Name two places he has visited and two things that he does or has done. Which of the jobs or activities are interesting to you? Tell your partner.

Who he is	What he does
Will Steger is an **explorer**.	He was the **leader** on a 1,200 mile (1,931 km) trip between Russia and Canada.
He is a **traveler**.	He was the first person to travel to both the North and South Poles by dogsled.
He is an **ambassador** for the planet.	He is a popular **speaker**. He talks about the changes in weather on the poles and around the world.
He is a **writer**.	He is the **author** of four books, including *Saving the Earth*.
He is a **teacher**.	He is the **founder** of the Steger Wilderness Center. He wants **educators** and **scientists** to come to the center. They can learn about the earth.

C Tell a partner about one or more famous people. Use three of the words in the chart below.

-ian	-or	-ist	-er
music**ian**	direct**or**	activ**ist**	research**er**
physic**ian**	doct**or**	journal**ist**	teach**er**
politic**ian**	instruct**or**	scient**ist**	travel**er**

> Jane Goodall is a famous scientist and researcher. She's also a popular speaker. She studies chimpanzees.

3 LISTENING

Canada

Costa Rica

Iceland

Antarctica

A   Look at the shaded places on the map. What do you know about these places?

B   🔊 **Infer information.** A radio announcer is interviewing Alejandro about his job. Listen to the interview and answer the question. **Track 14**

Where in the world is Alejandro? Circle it on the map.

C   🔊 **Listen for gist.** Listen again. What job(s) does Alejandro do? Circle your answer(s). **Track 14**

doctor   journalist   scientist   photographer   explorer   ski instructor

D   🔊 **Listen for details.** Listen again. What does Alejandro say?
Complete the sentences by circling the correct words. **Track 14**

1.   Sometimes my camera breaks / freezes.

2.   Today it's –13 / –30 degrees.

3.   I was born in Costa Rica / Canada.

4.   This place is very quiet / nice.

5.   I write for a newspaper / online.

E   🗣 Discuss the questions with a partner.

1.   Why is Alejandro's job dangerous?

2.   Is his job interesting to you? Why or why not?

3.   Can you name any other dangerous jobs?

4 SPEAKING

A 🔊 Listen to the conversation. Then follow the steps (1, 2) and answer the questions (3). **Track 15**

1. Find a word that means *not afraid*.

2. Find a word that means *a movie that shows real events.*

3. Do Kurt and Maggie like the movie? How do you know?

KURT: Hey, Maggie. What movie are you watching tonight?

MAGGIE: It's a documentary. It's called *Man on Wire*. It's my second time watching it.

KURT: *Man on Wire*... hmm....

MAGGIE: Do you know it?

KURT: Yeah, I do. It's a great movie.

MAGGIE: I agree. The guy in the movie was really brave.

KURT: Oh, I know. And it was in New York. I love New York City!

MAGGIE: Me, too. Hey, do you want to watch the movie with me?

KURT: Again? Well... sure. Why not?

B 🗣 Practice the conversation with a partner.

SPEAKING STRATEGY

C Complete the chart with information about two movies you like.

Name of movie	Actor(s) in movie	Words that describe movie

D 👥 In a group, talk about your movies. Use the Useful Expressions and the example to help you.

A: I think *Frozen* is a good movie.

B: Yeah, I agree. It's really fun.

C: Really? I don't think so.

B: Why do you say that?

C: I think the story is kind of boring.

Useful Expressions		
Agreeing or disagreeing with an opinion		
Statement: I think *Man on Wire* is a good movie.		**Follow-up questions**
Agreeing	I think so, too. I agree. Yeah, you're right.	What do you like about it?
Disagreeing	Really? I don't think so. Sorry, but I disagree. I don't really agree.	Why do you say that?
Speaking tip		
You can agree with a negative statement by saying *Me neither*. A: I don't like that movie. B: Me neither.		

5 GRAMMAR

A Turn to page 74. Complete the exercises. Then do **B–F** below.

Past Forms of *be*
am / is → **was**
am not / isn't → **wasn't**
are → **were**
aren't → **weren't**

The Simple Past Tense with *be*		
Affirmative and Negative Statements		
Subject	***was / were***	
I / He / She / It	**was / wasn't**	brave.
We / You / They	**were / weren't**	

Yes / No Questions			Answers
Was / Were	**Subject**		
Were	you	brave?	Yes, I **was**. / No, I **wasn't**.
Was	she		Yes, she **was**. / No, she **wasn't**.

Wh- Questions				Answers
***Wh-* word**	***was / were***	**Subject**		
When	**was**	he	born?	**Last** year. / A year **ago**. / **In** 2015.

B Use the words in the box to complete the chart. Pay attention to the verb forms in the chart.

ago	They
in	was
She	weren't
last	

Subject	*be*	
I / He / _____ / It	_____ / wasn't	there _____ 2007.
		on TV _____ night.
You / We / _____	were / _____	famous two years _____.

C Read about these explorers. Complete the sentences with simple past tense forms of *be*.

1963

Who (1.) _____ the first woman to fly in space?

Her name (2.) _____ Valentina Tereshkova.

She (3.) _____ Russian.

There (4.) _____ any other women in space for 19 years.

1980

Peng Jiamu (5.) _____ a famous scientist.

He (6.) _____ an explorer in the Lop Nur Desert of China.

He (7.) _____ lost in the desert in 1980.

His team members (8.) _____ able to find him. He was never seen again.

D Complete the chart with your birth year (1) and birthplace (2). Then complete 3–5 with information that was true about yourself *three years ago*.

	1. Birth year	2. Birthplace	3. Age	4. School	5. Best friend
Example	2001	Santiago	15	Colegio	Cesar
You					

E Interview two classmates. Ask them questions and complete the chart on p. 36 with their information.

the chart on p. 36 with their information.

> Where were you born?

> In the Dominican Republic.

F Share your information with another partner.

> This is Juan David. He was born in Santo Domingo. Three years ago, he was 15 years old.

> Were you born in Santo Domingo?

6 COMMUNICATION

A Read the headings in the chart. Then think of famous people you know and complete the chart. The people can be from the past or present. Share your answers with a partner.

Entertainers*	
Leaders	
Writers	
Explorers	
Activists	
(Other: your idea)	

* = singers, actors, musicians, etc.

B Use your information in **A** and follow the steps below.

1. You are going to have a dinner party. You can invite four famous people from the past or present.

2. Complete the chart with the names and jobs of the people you want to invite.

3. List your reasons for inviting them.

1. Person: Job: Reason:	
2. Person: Job: Reason:	
3. Person: Job: Reason:	
4. Person: Job: Reason:	

C Get into a group of three people. Compare your answers in **B**. Explain your choices. Together, make one list of four people to invite to the party.

> I think we should invite Junko Tabei. She was the first woman to climb Mount Everest.

> I agree. Let's invite her.

Knicole Colón: astronomer
(a scientist who studies space)
and National Geographic Explorer

As a kid, who was your role-model?
At age 12, I saw the movie *Contact*. In the movie, there's a woman named Ellie. She works as an astronomer, and she's looking for life on other planets. She's very smart. She's brave, too. She travels to space alone. She was only a character in a movie, but I really looked up to her! I also really admire the astronomer Galileo Galilei. He's my hero, too.

1 VOCABULARY

A Read the definition. Then circle the words that can complete the sentence below.
Look up any new words.

> A *role-model* is someone you *admire*. You think the person is great. You want to be like the person. What words describe a role-model?

Word Bank
admire = look up to (someone)
role-model = hero

A role-model is a _____ person.

brave	confused	hardworking	nervous
confident	generous	kind	smart / intelligent

B 🔁 Read the interview with Knicole Colón. Then answer the questions with a partner.

1. What does Knicole Colón do?
2. As a kid, who was her hero?
3. Why did Knicole look up to this person?
4. Who else does Knicole admire?

C Complete the sentences. Use words in **A** to describe the person.

I admire _____. I look up to this person because _____.

Jack Andraka is an inventor.

Lydia Ko is a golf player.

A 🔄 Look at the words in the Word Bank. Then read the photo captions. What do these two people do? Tell a partner.

Word Bank
cancer = a very serious disease
die = to stop living
invent = to be first to make something
tool = a handheld item used for work

B 🔊 **Listen for gist.** Listen to a profile of each person. Check the best title for each. **Track 16**

1. ☐ Jack Andraka: Brave Teenage Doctor

   ☐ Jack Andraka: Smart Scientist

2. ☐ Lydia Ko: Hardworking Athlete

   ☐ Lydia Ko: Generous Golf Player

C 🔊 **Listen for details.** Listen again. Complete the sentences with a word or number. **Track 16**

1. When Jack was _____, his friend died of cancer.

2. Jack was very _____.

3. At age _____, he invented a _____.

4. It helps doctors find certain cancers _____.

5. Lydia started playing golf at age _____.

6. She practiced to be the _____.

7. By age _____, she was the number _____ women's golf player.

8. For years, golf was mostly a _____ sport. Now, more _____ want to play.

D 🔄 Do you admire Jack and Lydia? Why or why not? Tell a partner.

3 READING 🔊 Track 17

A 🔄 **Make predictions; Infer information.**
Look at the photos on the next page. Sanga Moses invented something. What is it? Tell a partner.

B **Read for details.** Read paragraphs 1 and 2. Then complete the sentences.

1. In Uganda, many people use _____ to cook.

2. This makes the air _____.

3. Many children don't go to _____.

4. Sanga Moses's company invented a new _____.

5. It changes extra or unused _____ parts into fuel.

C **Sequence events.** Read the first question and answer in the reading. Then put the events in order from 1 to 6.

_____ Sanga Moses decided to fix the problem.

_____ He talked to his sister.

_____ He stopped working at the bank.

_____ Sanga Moses visited his mother.

_____ He started Eco-Fuel Africa.

_____ She cried because she missed school to get wood.

D **Read for details.** Read the second question and answer in the reading. Complete the sentence and the four reasons.

Sanga Moses's invention is / isn't helping people.

1. Women are making _____.

2. The air is _____.

3. People are saving _____.

4. Girls can stay in _____.

E 🔄 Work with a partner. Use your answers in **B–D** to answer the questions.

1. What was the problem in Uganda?

2. What did Sanga Moses do about the problem?

3. Do you admire Sanga Moses? Why or why not?

ECO-FUEL AFRICA

One company is changing people's lives in Uganda.

In Uganda, many people use wood for fuel.[1] But using wood makes the air dirty. Also many children—usually girls—don't go to school. They spend hours getting the wood for cooking.

But now things are changing. Sanga Moses started a company called Eco-Fuel Africa. The company invented a new kind of oven. It changes extra or unused food parts into fuel. This kind of fuel is clean (unlike wood). Here, Sanga Moses answers two questions about his company.

Why did you start Eco-Fuel Africa?

Sanga Moses: In January 2009, I worked in a big bank in Kampala (the capital of Uganda). One day, I visited my mother in my home village. Going home, I met my 12-year-old sister on the road. She carried a lot of wood. My sister started crying. She didn't go to school that day because she walked for ten kilometers to get wood for my family. I was very unhappy about this. I wanted my sister to stay in school. That day, I decided to fix[2] this problem. I stopped working at the bank, and I started Eco-Fuel Africa.

Is Eco-Fuel Africa helping people?

Sanga Moses: Yes, I think so. For example, we have a group of 460 women. They use our ovens to make clean cooking fuel. Then they sell it. Each woman makes $150 a month in extra money. And about 115,000 people use our clean cooking fuel in Uganda. Today, the air is cleaner, and we are saving trees. And best of all, girls can stay in school.

[1]*Fuel* is something like wood or oil. People use fuel to make energy for cooking food and other activities.
[2]If something doesn't work and you *fix* it, you make it work.

Sanga Moses (right) and a new kind of oven are helping people in Uganda.

Children find wood for their families.

4 GRAMMAR See pages 81–82 for practice with irregular simple past verbs and questions.

A Turn to pages 75–76. Complete the exercises. Then do **B–E** below.

The Simple Past: Affirmative and Negative Statements		
I / You / He / She / We / They	visit**ed** / didn't visit	Tokyo.
I / You / He / She / We / They	start**ed** / didn't start	a company.

move → move**d**
start → start**ed**
study → stud**ied**
stop → stop**ped**

B 🔊 **Pronunciation: Past tense -ed endings.**
Listen to these past tense verbs. Say each word with the speaker. Pay attention to the pronunciation of the -ed ending. **Track 18**

/t/	/d/	/ɪd/
liked, stopped	moved, tried	visited, waited

C 🔊 🔁 **Pronunciation: Past tense -ed endings.** How is the -ed sound said in each verb? Listen and circle your answer. Then say the words with a partner. **Track 19**

1. walked   /t/   /ɪd/
2. started   /d/   /ɪd/
3. wanted   /d/   /ɪd/
4. returned   /d/   /ɪd/
5. asked   /t/   /ɪd/
6. cried   /d/   /ɪd/
7. listened   /d/   /ɪd/
8. needed   /t/   /ɪd/
9. finished   /t/   /ɪd/

D 🔁 Work with a partner. Complete Alec's story with simple past tense verbs. Then take turns reading the story aloud. Pay attention to pronunciation.

Help from a Stranger

There was a girl named Alyssa in my class. I (1. like) _____ her a lot. One day, I (2. invite) _____ her to have dinner with me at a restaurant.

At the end, I (3. ask) _____ the waiter for the check. I (4. offer) _____ to pay. I (5. look) _____ in my wallet, but I only had ten dollars. I (6. not have) _____ enough money!

I left the table. I (7. try) _____ to call my roommate. I (8. wait) _____, but my roommate (9. not answer) _____ his phone. I left a message and (10. explain) _____ my problem.

Just then, the door (11. open) _____. It was my waiter. He (12. hand) _____ me $40. I (13. promise) _____ to pay him back. He (14. reply) _____, "Don't worry about it." What a kind and generous guy!

E 🔁 Ask and answer the questions with a partner.

1. Where were Alec and Alyssa?
2. What happened after dinner?
3. When Alec realized his problem, what did he do?
4. Who helped Alec?
5. What did Alec promise?
6. What did the waiter reply?

5 WRITING

A Read the paragraph. Complete the sentences with simple past tense verbs.

My Hero

My hero is my grandmother. I admire her a lot. She is very smart and hardworking. At age 35, she (1. start) _____ her own business. She (2. own) _____ a small store. At first, she (3. not know) _____ a lot about business, but she (4. work) _____ hard, and she (5. learn) _____ fast. In time, her store (6. be) _____ successful. She (7. hire) _____ five people. I also (8. help) _____ her in the summers. I (9. learn) _____ a lot about business from my grandmother. Now my grandmother is 74 years old. Two years ago, she (10. close) _____ her store, but she is still busy. She travels and she sees her friends. She is a great woman!

B 🗘 Check your answers in **A** with a partner. Then answer the questions.

1. Who does the writer admire?
2. Why? What did the person do?
3. The writer uses adjectives to describe his hero. What are they?

C Who is your hero? Answer the questions in **B** about your person. Then use your notes and the model in **A** to help you write your own paragraph.

D 🗘 Share your writing with a partner. Circle any mistakes and answer the questions in **B**. Then return the paper to your partner. Make corrections to your own paragraph.

6 COMMUNICATION

A Every year, there are three choices for the Hero of the Year award. Read about this year's three choices. Which person is your choice? Why?

Jason Yang, 30

Five years ago, Jason Yang started his own company. Today, he is a millionaire. This year he is giving ten poor children $10,000 each for college.

Amanda Garcia, 54

A month ago, there was a car fire near Amanda Garcia's house. A child was in the car. Amanda pulled the child from the car. She saved the little boy's life.

Logan Myers, 22

When he was 16, Logan Myers was in a car accident. Now he is in a wheelchair. This year, he climbed 3,776 meters to the top of Mount Fuji using special ropes. Now Logan is preparing for his next challenge: Mount Everest.

B 👥 Get into a group of three or four people. Explain your choice to the group. Then together choose one person to get the award. Explain your answer to the class.

> I admire Logan. He's very brave and...

4 AT THE MOVIES

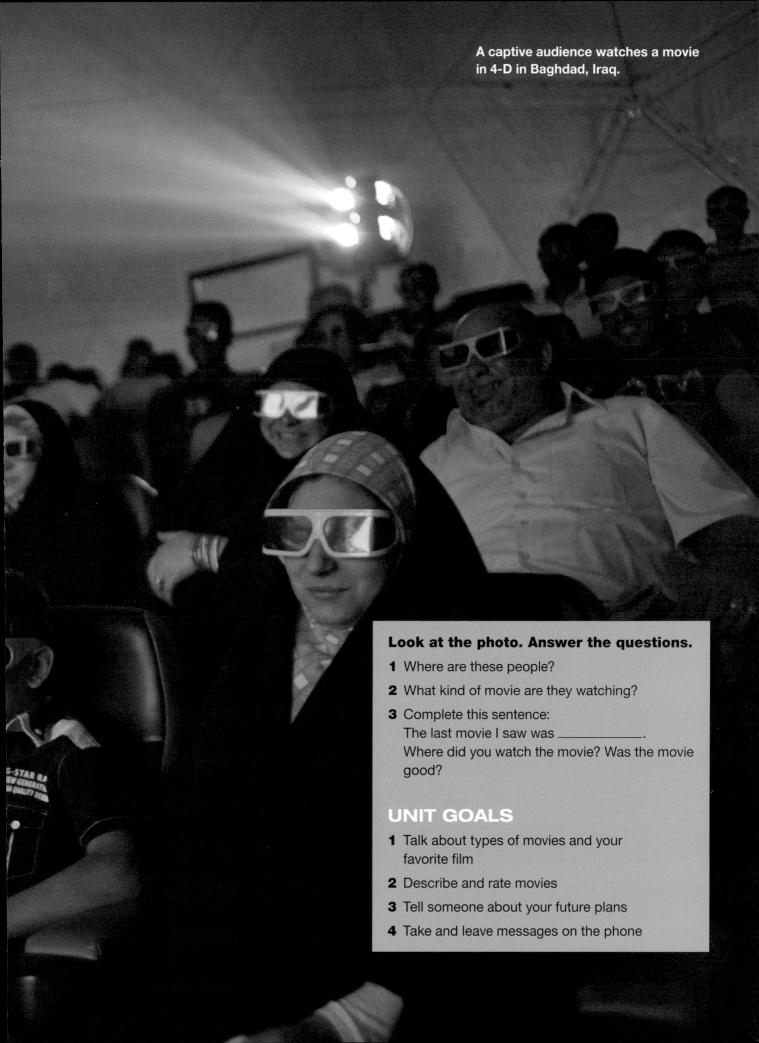

A captive audience watches a movie in 4-D in Baghdad, Iraq.

Look at the photo. Answer the questions.

1 Where are these people?

2 What kind of movie are they watching?

3 Complete this sentence:
The last movie I saw was _____.
Where did you watch the movie? Was the movie good?

UNIT GOALS

1 Talk about types of movies and your favorite film

2 Describe and rate movies

3 Tell someone about your future plans

4 Take and leave messages on the phone

1 **VIDEO** Spider-Man in Real Life

A Look at the photo. Do you know this character? What does he do?

B ▶ A group of people are creating a Spider-Man movie scene in real life. They are on top of a tall building in New York City.

1. Read the sentences below. Put the events in order from 1–6.
2. Watch the video and check your answers.

___ People on the street see Spider-Man.   ___ Spider-Man and the woman fly away together.

___ Spider-Man jumps off the building.   ___ Spider-Man fights the bad guy.

___ The woman thanks Spider-Man.   ___ A woman needs help.

C ▶ Read the sentences. Then watch again and circle the best answer(s). Sometimes more than one answer is possible.

1. When the people on the street see the woman, they are excited / happy / worried.
2. When Spider-Man jumps off the building, the people on the street are shocked / scared / happy.
3. When Spider-Man flies away, the people on the street are worried / happy / confused.

D 🔗 Do you know any Spider-Man movies? Do you like them? Why or why not? Tell a partner.

2 VOCABULARY

A 🔁 Talk with a partner. Answer the questions.

1. Look at the movie posters. Practice saying each type of movie. What is your favorite kind of movie? Why?

2. Read about each one. Which one do you want to see? Why?

3. Which kinds of movies **make you** laugh? cry? think? scream?

4. Do you prefer a movie with a happy ending? Why or why not?

musical / drama
Four young men come together and create a singing group…

romantic comedy
At first, Rosie and Alex were friends…

action movie
James Bond fights the bad guys…

science fiction thriller
The Robinson family is in outer space and needs to get home…

horror film
A teenager has a strange new neighbor…

classic / old movie
A young woman living in New York meets a writer in her building and…

3 LISTENING

A 🔊 **Pronunciation: Syllable stress.** Say the words. Then listen and repeat. Which syllable is stressed in each one? Underline it. **Track 20**

romantic   comedy   documentary   musical

B 💬 **Make predictions.** The words on the left describe movies. What do you think they mean? Discuss with a partner.

1. tearjerker
2. chick flick
3. blockbuster
4. indie

a. a successful movie that costs a lot to make
b. a less famous movie that costs less to make
c. a movie that makes you cry
d. a scary movie that is not good for children
e. a romantic movie that is popular with women

C 🔊 **Check predictions.** Listen to a man and woman discuss movies. Match the words above to their definitions. One definition is extra. **Track 21**

D 🔊 **Listen for details.** Listen again. How do the man and woman talk about likes and dislikes? Complete the sentences. **Track 21**

1. "I'm _____ movies about love and romance."
2. "I thought you were _____ action movies!"
3. "Sorry, but I'm _____ horror films either."

Word Bank
Talking about likes and dislikes
(not) crazy about   *(not) a big fan of*   *(not) into*

E 💬 Complete the chart with one example of each type of movie. Then compare your list with a partner's. Tell your partner about one of the movies from your list.

tearjerker	
chick flick	
blockbuster	
indie	

At film festivals, like Sundance, reviewers and fans have the chance to see many movies in one place.

4 SPEAKING

A 🔊 Listen to the conversation. Take a phone message for Michael. Complete the information in the box. **Track 22**

PAM: Hello?

SILVIO: Hi. Is Michael there, please?

PAM: Who's calling?

SILVIO: This is Silvio, a friend from school.

PAM: OK. Hang on a minute.

SILVIO: Thanks.

PAM: Hello? Sorry. Michael's not here. Can I take a message?

SILVIO: Yeah. We're going to a movie tonight. I have an extra ticket for Michael.

PAM: OK. What time does it start?

SILVIO: In a half hour from now—at 8:00.

PAM: All right. I'll give him the message.

SILVIO: Thanks a lot.

B 🔁 Practice the conversation with a partner.

SPEAKING STRATEGY

C Think of a movie that you want to see with a friend. Then answer the questions to complete the chart.

What is the name of the movie?	Time	Place	What is your friend's name?

D 🔁 With your partner, play one of these roles in a phone conversation. Use the Useful Expressions to help you.

Student A: You call your friend to invite him or her to a movie. Your friend isn't home. Leave a message with a family member.

Student B: Answer the phone. Take a message. Fill out the note on the right.

E 🔁 Switch roles and practice again.

While You Were Out

Time of Call: _____

_____ called.

Movie is at _____. He has _____ for you.

Word Bank

hang on = please wait

Useful Expressions

Taking and leaving a message

Hello? Is Michael there?

  Who's calling, please?

This is Silvio.

  OK. Hang on a minute.

  Sorry. Michael's not home yet / not here. Can I take a message?

While You Were Out

Time of Call: _____

Name of Caller: _____

Message: _____

_____

---

5 GRAMMAR See page 83 for practice with "be going to" for future tense.

A Turn to pages 76–77. Complete the exercise. Then do **B–D** below.

The Present Continuous as Future			
Subject + *be*	**Verb + *ing***		**Future time expressions**
We're	seeing	a movie	today / tonight / tomorrow. in an hour. this weekend.
They're	making		next year.

B Complete the time expressions with a word from the box. One item does not need a word.

> in   the   this / next

1. _____ day after tomorrow
2. _____ month

3. _____ tonight
4. _____ a few days

C Work with a partner. Four of the sentences below correctly use the present continuous tense to talk about future plans, but two sentences do not. Cross out the two incorrect sentences.

1. We're seeing a movie later today.
2. I'm meeting them in front of the theater at 2:00.
3. We're having a lot of snow next week.
4. They're watching the Oscars tonight.
5. You need to rest or you're getting sick.
6. We're going out of town this weekend.

> **i** Events that you <u>can</u> plan: a vacation, meeting friends on the weekend
> Events that you <u>cannot</u> plan: the weather, illness
> Do not use the present continuous as future for events that you <u>cannot</u> plan.

D Look at the sentences you didn't cross out in **C**. Work with a partner to make a short conversation using at least three of the sentences.

People lining up outside of the Oscars

6 COMMUNICATION

A Work in a small group. You are going to create a poster for a new movie. Follow the steps below.

1. Write the names of two people in your movie.

   famous actor: _____   famous actress: _____

2. Choose one of the following to appear in your movie.

   a monster   a superhero   a cowboy

   an alien   a spy   your idea: _____

3. Choose a location for your movie: _____

4. What kind of movie is it? Circle one.

   action movie   horror film   sci-fi thriller

   drama   romantic comedy   other: _____

5. Finally, choose a title for your movie: _____

B Now make the poster advertising your movie. Put your group's poster on the wall.

C Walk around and look at all the posters. Which movie do you want to see? Invite two people to see the movie with you.

> *The Monster Next Door* looks really good.

> It does. I'm a big fan of scary movies. They make me scream!

> Me too. Hey, I'm seeing it tonight at 7:00. Do you want to come?

> Sorry, but I can't. I'm going to a different movie then.

A scene from a Bollywood film

1 VOCABULARY

A 🔲 The people below watched different movies recently.

1. Take turns with a partner. Read each opinion aloud.

2. Did the person like the movie? Why or why not?

Word Bank
Word Partnerships
You can **go to** / **see** / **watch** a movie.

> I watched *The Hunger Games*.
> It was very **suspenseful**.
> I kept thinking, "What's going to happen next?"

> I watched a Bollywood movie.
> It was really **entertaining**. There was a lot of singing and dancing, and it was a **sweet** love story, too. It was a lot of fun.

> You need to see *Invictus*. It's about a rugby team from South Africa. It's very **inspiring**. You feel good and you think about life, too.

> I saw a **depressing** movie last weekend. It was so sad that I stopped watching it.

> I saw a **hilarious** movie last night. The comic in it was really funny.

> I watched this **scary** zombie movie with my boyfriend. He's crazy about them, but for me, they're too **violent**. There's too much blood!

B 🔲 Now think of movies you know. Tell your partner your ideas.

Name a(n) _____ movie.

1. suspenseful	3. inspiring	5. entertaining	7. scary
2. hilarious	4. depressing	6. sweet	8. violent

2 LISTENING

A 🔄 Read the definitions in the Word Bank. Then answer the questions. Tell a partner.

1. Where do you usually see movie trailers?

   online   on TV   at the movies

2. What movie is coming out soon? Name one.

> A new *Star Wars* movie is coming out this year.

B 🔊 **Listen for a speaker's opinion.** A man and woman are talking about movies. Listen and circle the correct opinion (1a–6a) below. **Track 23**

Word Bank
A *movie trailer* is an ad. It shows some scenes from a movie.
When a movie *comes out*, it is available to watch.

Opinion

1a. The woman likes / dislikes the *Fast Cars* movies.

2a. The man likes / dislikes the *Fast Cars* movies.

3a. The woman likes / dislikes actress Laura Swift.

4a. The man likes / dislikes Laura Swift.

5a. The woman wants / doesn't want to see Laura Swift's new movie.

6a. The man wants / doesn't want to see Laura Swift's new movie.

Reason

1b. They are good stories / violent.

2b. They are entertaining / hilarious.

3b. She is / isn't funny.

4b. She is / isn't funny.

5b. Her new movie sounds sad / hilarious.

6b. Her new movie is funny / inspiring.

C 🔊 **Listen for details.** What reason does each person give? Listen again and circle the correct reason (1b–6b) in **B**. **Track 23**

D 🔊 **Listen for details.** Listen again. Circle T for *true* and F for *false.* If a sentence is false, make it true. **Track 23**

1. *Fast Cars 4* is an action movie.   T   F

2. *Fast Cars 4* is coming out next week.   T   F

3. Laura Swift's new movie is a comedy.   T   F

4. In her new movie, Laura Swift is a rich woman in London.   T   F

E 🔄 With a partner, take turns asking the questions about the two movies you heard about.

1. What kind of movie is it?

2. Do you like these kinds of movies? Why or why not?

> What kind of movie is Fast Cars 4?

3 READING 🔊 Track 24

A **Use background knowledge.** Look at the reading. One movie is the original; the other is a *remake* (a new version of an old film). Do you know any movie remakes?

B **Make predictions.** Look at the photos. Guess the answer to the question.

What words describe the movie *Shutter*?

a. hilarious   c. inspiring

b. scary   d. suspenseful

C **Check predictions.** Read the movie descriptions. Check your answer(s) in **B**.

What information in the reading helped you confirm or change your answer(s)? Underline it.

D **Read for details.** Which movie does each sentence describe? Check *original*, *remake*, or *both*.

1. The man's name is Tun.
   ☐ original   ☐ remake

2. The man is a photographer.
   ☐ original   ☐ remake

3. There is a car accident.
   ☐ original   ☐ remake

4. They see a girl in the photos.
   ☐ original   ☐ remake

5. The story takes place in Japan.
   ☐ original   ☐ remake

6. The critics didn't like this movie.
   ☐ original   ☐ remake

E 🔁 Answer the questions with a partner.

1. Would you like to see this movie—either the original or the remake? Why or why not?

2. What movies should not be remade?

A MOVIE REMAKE

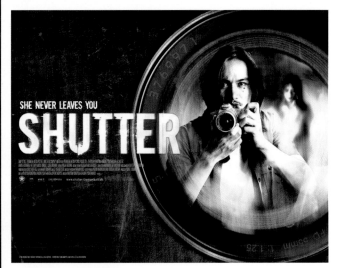

SHUTTER (original)

In this popular film from Thailand, Tun, a photographer, and his girlfriend, Jane, are driving home on a lonely country road one night. Suddenly they see a girl in the road. Jane tries to stop the car, but it's too late. She hits and kills the girl. Feeling very afraid, Tun and Jane leave the girl and quickly drive back home to Bangkok.

Jane and Tun try to return to normal life, but then strange things start happening. Tun starts to have bad neck pain. And both Jane and Tun see strange images in Tun's photographs. They look like a girl. Is it the girl on the road?

[1]A movie *critic* watches movies and gives an opinion about them.
[2]If a movie *flops*, it isn't successful.

SHUTTER (remake)

This movie is an American remake of a Thai movie with the same name. The critics[1] thought the film would flop,[2] but it did well and made over $45 million worldwide.

The main characters are Jane and her husband Ben. They move to Tokyo for Ben's new job as a photographer. One night they are in a car accident on a country road. They hit a young girl and drive into a tree. When they wake up, they look for the girl, but they can't find her. Was the girl really there?

Jane and Ben try to forget the frightening experience, but they can't. Then Ben's shoulder starts to hurt all the time. And when Ben looks at his photos, there are strange lights in them. Ben's helper, Seiko, thinks the lights look like a girl. Is it the girl on the road?

4 GRAMMAR

A   Turn to pages 77–78. Complete the exercises. Then do **B–D** below.

-ed Adjectives	-ing Adjectives
I'm **bored**. I don't like this movie.	This movie is **boring**. Let's watch something else.

B   Read the conversation. Complete each sentence with the correct adjective. Then work in a group of three and practice the conversation.

A: What did you do this weekend?

B: Not much. Mostly I watched movies.

C: What did you see?

A: I saw *Midnight on the Moon*. It was good. I was surprised / surprising.

B: Really? I saw that movie, too. I was kind of bored / boring by it.

A: You're kidding. It was amazed / amazing.

B: In my opinion, it was kind of slow and depressed / depressing in places.

A: Did you see the movie, Juan?

C: Yeah, I did.

A: What did you think?

C: Well, parts of the movie were bored / boring, but mostly it was entertained / entertaining. And the ending was excited / exciting.

A: I thought so, too!

C   In the same group, think of a movie you all saw. Then, on your own, use *-ed* / *-ing* adjectives to give your opinion of the movie.

A movie we all saw: _____

My opinion of the movie: _____

How I felt watching it (use an *-ed* adjective): _____

How the movie was (use an *-ing* adjective): _____

D   Use the conversation in **B** and your ideas in **C** to talk about your movie.

5 WRITING

A   Read about one person's favorite movie. Answer the questions with a partner.

1. What is the writer's favorite movie?

2. What kind of movie is it? What is it about?

3. What happens in the movie?

My Favorite Movie

My favorite movie of all time is *Cinema Paradiso*. It's a classic film from the 1980s. It's about an Italian boy named Salvatore. He loves movies.

In the film, Salvatore remembers his childhood. When he was young, he watched movies at the Cinema Paradiso, a theater in his hometown. He had an old friend named Alfredo, and he loved a girl named Elena. The movie is about these people's lives. It is a very sweet and inspiring film. You should see it!

Cinema Paradiso is *set* in Palazzo Adriano, Italy. Where a movie is set is where it takes place.

B Answer the questions in **A** about your favorite movie. Write your ideas in a few words.

C Write two paragraphs about your movie. Use your notes in **B**.

- Paragraph 1: Say the name of the movie, the kind of movie it is, and what it's about.
- Paragraph 2: Explain what happens in the movie.
- In your writing, use adjectives from this lesson.
- End with a short sentence. Tell people to see the movie.

D Exchange papers with a partner.

1. Answer the questions in **A** about your partner's movie.

2. Circle mistakes in your partner's writing. Then return the paper to him or her.

E Make corrections to your writing. Then put together a "Must-See Movies" list with all of your classmates' ideas.

6 COMMUNICATION

A Prepare a short talk about your favorite movie.

1. Practice: Use your notes from Writing to talk about it.

2. Find a short movie trailer to use in your presentation.

B Work in a group of four. Give your presentation.

When you listen, take notes. Answer the questions in Writing **A** about your partners' movies.

C Your group talked about four movies. What do you think of each one?

Use the sentences below to tell your group.

I saw _____,...

☐ and I liked it because...

☐ but I didn't like it because...

I did not see _____,...

☐ but now I'd like to see it.

☐ and I don't plan to see it.

> I saw *Thor*, but I didn't like it. I'm not into movies about comic book characters.

1 STORYBOARD

A Lisa and Eva are roommates. Look at the pictures and work with a partner to complete the conversations. More than one answer is possible for most blanks.

B Practice the conversations with a partner. Then change roles and practice again.

2 SEE IT AND SAY IT

A  Describe a person in the picture below to your partner. Don't say the person's name. Your partner guesses the person.

> This person has long hair and...

B Talk about the picture with a partner.

- Where are the people?
- What are they doing?
- Which people are meeting for the first time? How do you know?
- Ask one question about the picture.

C Choose one pair or group of people. With a partner, role-play a conversation of five to six sentences between the people.

> Hi, I'm Felipe.

> Hi, Felipe. Nice to meet you. My name is...

3 ODD WORD OUT

A Look at the words. Circle the one that is different in each group.

1. nervous   embarrassed   angry   happy
2. grapes   carrots   onions   lettuce
3. red   gray   curly   black
4. cheese   yogurt   milk   orange juice
5. heavy   short   slim   thin
6. point at   bark at   wave to   talk to
7. Japan   Portuguese   Chinese   English

B 🔁 Compare and explain your answers with a partner.

> For number 1, happy is different. It's a good feeling. Nervous, embarrassed, and angry are bad feelings.

4 DO YOU EVER…?

A Read each question. Answer *Yes* or *No*. Then write a sentence to give some extra information. Use the correct pronouns for the underlined words.

1. Do you give your mom flowers?

   Yes. I give her flowers on her birthday.

2. Does your mom speak to your dad in English?

   _____

3. Do you eat vegetables?

   _____

4. Do your friends send you text messages?

   _____

5. Does your instructor give you and your classmates homework?

   _____

6. Do you and your friends give your homework to your instructor late?

   _____

B 🔁 Ask your partner the questions in **A**. Listen to his or her answers. Then ask your partner one more question.

> Does your mom speak to your dad in English?

> No, she always speaks to him in Spanish.

> Does he understand English?

> No, not really.

5 LISTENING: THE PERFECT DIET?

A 🔊 Tino and Mary are talking about Tino's diet. Listen and circle your answers.
Track 25

1. Which sentence is true?

   a. Mary thinks Tino eats too much.
   b. Tino is worried about his health.
   c. Mary thinks Tino's diet is too unhealthy.
   d. Tino is worried about Mary's health.

2. What is Tino NOT eating?

   a. protein
   b. vegetables
   c. fruit
   d. vitamins

B 🔊 Listen again. Which foods can he eat? Check the boxes. **Track 25**

C Is Tino's diet healthy? Why or why not? Tell a partner.

6 TALK ABOUT...

A Get into a group of three people. Follow the steps below.

1. One person chooses a topic from the list and says it to the group.

   - your hobbies
   - why you are learning English
   - your favorite music
   - a country you want to visit
   - your favorite TV show
   - your favorite food
   - your best friend
   - something you don't like

   > My topic is "your hobbies."

   > What do you do for fun?

2. Each person in the group asks the first person a question about the topic. That person answers each question.

3. Take turns and repeat steps 1 and 2 for each topic.

7 STORYBOARD

A  Vivian and Jun are visiting a museum. Complete the conversation with a partner. Sometimes more than one answer is possible.

B Practice the conversation with a partner. Then switch roles and practice again.

8 SEE IT AND SAY IT

A 🔁 Look at the photos. Answer the questions about each place with a partner. Complete the sentence.

1. What season does this look like?

2. How's the weather?

3. What's the temperature?

4. In Punta Cana, it's _____, but in Harbin it's _____.

Punta Cana, Dominican Republic
85°F/29°c

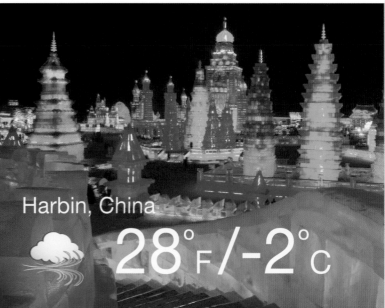

Harbin, China
28°F/-2°c

B 🔁 Your partner is going on vacation to one of the places above. What should he or she pack? Use ideas in the box and one of your own. Explain your choices.

a camera	boots
a coat	sandals
a hat	shorts
a swimsuit	sunscreen
an umbrella	my idea: _____

Student A: You're going to Punta Cana.

Student B: You're going to Harbin.

> It's very cold there now, so I think you should pack a coat.

> Good idea. I will.

9 MEMORY GAME

A   Play a memory game with a partner. Read the instructions below.

Player A: Study the words and numbers in the chart below for 15 seconds. Then close your book and draw the chart on a piece of paper. Fill in as many words and numbers as you can remember.

Player B: Check Player A's answers.

cloudy	68
fall asleep	go sightseeing
whose	get up
529	admire
passport	musician

B   Play the game again. Switch roles. Use the chart below.

journalist	raining
explorer	memory
313	mine
should	wake up
47	unpack

C   Answer the questions with a partner.

1. How many words did you remember?
2. Which words did you forget?
3. Which words were easy to remember? Why?

D   Choose four words from each chart and write sentences using them. At least two sentences should be in the past tense.

E   Tell a partner your sentences. Then your partner asks you one question about each sentence.

Yesterday, I fell asleep early.

When did you go to bed?

10 LISTEN: QUESTIONS AND ANSWERS

A 🔊 You will hear a question and then four answers about each photo. Circle the letter that best answers the question. **Track 26**

1.

   A   B   C   D

2.

   A   B   C   D

3.

   A   B   C   D

11 SPEAK FOR A MINUTE!

A Read the questions and think about your answers.

1. What's your favorite season? Why? What's the weather like?

2. Where did you go on your last vacation? How did you prepare for the trip?

3. Describe your early years (from birth to age five).

4. What are two interesting jobs?

   I was born in...

5. Who do you admire?

6. Talk about a time when you forgot something. What happened?

B 👥 Get into a group of three.

1. Take turns. Choose a question from **A**.

2. Answer the question by talking for one minute without stopping and you get one point.

3. Continue until there are no more questions.

4. The winner is the person with the most points.

UNIT 1 PEOPLE

LESSON A

Vocabulary

born in
city
contact information
email address
favorites
first / last name
friends
hometown
interested in
job
languages
phone number
subject

Speaking Strategy

Introducing Yourself
A: My name is Mariana.
B: Hi, I'm Danny. (It's) Nice to meet you.
A: (It's) Nice to meet you, too.

Asking about Occupations
A: What do you do?
B: I'm a music student.

LESSON B

Vocabulary

Use *be* with…	Use *have* with…
Age	**Eye color**
young	**(dark) brown**
in his / her teens*	**blue**
	green
in his / her twenties*	**Hairstyle**
elderly (80+)	**long ↔ short**
	straight ↔ curly
Weight	**wavy**
skinny	**spiky**
thin	
slim**	**Hair color**
average weight	**black**
heavy	**(light / dark) brown**
Height	**blond**
short	**red**
average	**gray**
tall	
	Facial hair
	beard
	mustache

*teens (13–19), twenties (ages 20–29), thirties, forties, etc.
**Slim* means *skinny / thin*, but *slim* has a positive meaning.

LESSON A

Vocabulary

asking
barking
helping
looking
meeting
pointing
running
saying
shouting
sitting
smiling
talking
walking
waving to

Speaking Strategy

Greeting people and asking how they are

☺ A: Hi, _____. How's it going?
B: Fine. / OK. / All right. / Pretty good. / Not bad. How about you?
A: I'm fine, thanks.

☹ A: Hi, _____. How are you doing?
B: So-so. / Not so good.
A: Really? What's wrong?
B: I'm (a little) worried. / I'm (kind of) tired. I have a big test tomorrow.

LESSON B

Vocabulary

<u>Feelings</u>
angry
bored
confused
confident
embarrassed
excited
happy
nervous / **worried**
relaxed
sad

<u>Gestures / Actions</u>
bow
kiss
press noses together
shake hands

UNIT 3 HEROES

LESSON A

Vocabulary

activist
ambassador
author
director
doctor
educator
explorer
founder
instructor
journalist
leader
musician
physician
politician
researcher
scientist
speaker
teacher
traveler
writer

brave
documentary

Speaking Strategy

Agreeing or disagreeing with an opinion

I think *Man on Wire* is a good movie.
  I think so, too.
  I agree.
  Yeah, you're right.

  Really? I don't think so.
  Sorry, but I disagree.
  I don't really agree.

What do you like about it?
Why do you say that?

LESSON B

Vocabulary

admire / **look up to** (someone)
generous
hardworking
kind
look for (something or someone)
role model / **hero**
smart / intelligent
work as (a doctor / scientist)

cancer
die / died
invent / invented
tool

UNIT **4** **AT THE MOVIES**

LESSON A

Vocabulary

action movie
blockbuster
chick flick
classic / old movie
documentary
drama
horror film
indie
musical
romantic comedy
science fiction (sci-fi) thriller
tearjerker

make you (laugh / cry / think / scream)

(not) a (big) fan of (something)
(not) crazy about (something)
(not) into (something)

Speaking Strategy

Taking and leaving a message
Hello? Is Michael there?
　Who's calling, please?
This is Silvio.
　OK. Hang on a minute.
　Sorry. Michael's not home yet / not here. Can I take a message?

LESSON B

Vocabulary

depressing
entertaining
hilarious
inspiring
scary
suspenseful
sweet
violent
go / **see** / **watch** a movie

GRAMMAR NOTES

UNIT **1** PEOPLE

LESSON A

Review of the Simple Present Tense							
Affirmative statements				**Negative statements**			
I / You / We / They	speak	English.		I / You / We / They	don't	speak	English.
He / She / It	speaks			He / She / It	doesn't		

Yes / No* questions with *be				**Short answers**		
Is	she	a	student?	Yes, she **is**.	No, she's not.* / No, she **isn't**.	
Are	you			Yes, I **am**.	No, I'm not.	
	they		students?	Yes, they **are**.	No, they're not.* / No, they **aren't**.	

*In spoken English, this negative form is more common.

***Yes / No* questions with other verbs**				**Short answers**	
Do	you	speak	English?	Yes, I **do**.	No, I **don't**.
Does	she			Yes, she **does**.	No, she **doesn't**.

***Wh-* questions**				**Short answers**	
Where	do	you	live?	I live in Buenos Aires.	
	does	he		He still lives in his hometown.	
What	do	you	do?	I'm a student.	
	does	she		She's a doctor.	

A Complete the questions and answers. Then match each question to an appropriate answer.

1. _____ you live alone?

2. _____ _____ you do for fun?

3. _____ you a good student?

4. _____ _____ you live with?

5. _____ you a teacher?

6. _____ is your part-time job?

a. No, _____ _____. I'm a student.

b. My mother and father.

c. Yes, _____ _____. I get good grades.

d. I'm in a band.

e. I'm an office clerk.

f. No, I _____. I live with my family.

LESSON B

Describing Appearance			
Subject	***be / have***	**Adjective**	**Noun**
He	**is**	tall.	
		average	height / weight.
		young / in his teens.	
	has	blue	eyes.
		short, black	hair.

Use *be* to describe a person's height, weight, and age.

Use *have* to describe a person's eye color, hairstyle and color, and facial hair.

   *The exceptions: He **is** bald. (He has no hair on his head.)

                    He **is** clean-shaven. (He has no hair on his face.)

When using two or more adjectives, the words usually follow this pattern:

length / size—style—color

He has **short, curly, red** hair.   She has **big blue** eyes.

A   Complete the sentences with the correct form of *be* or *have*.

1. Tanya's dad _____ average height.

2. Ricardo and his sister _____ wavy hair.

3. My grandmother _____ in her eighties. She _____ elderly.

4. I _____ green eyes.

5. Max and Charlie are brothers. Max _____ a beard and mustache.
   Charlie _____ clean-shaven. They both _____ blond hair.

6. Damon _____ heavy. He weighs 150 kilos.

B   Look at the photo and make sentences about the woman. Describe her appearance.

Name: Lupita Nyong'o

Job: Actress

Nationality: Kenyan, Mexican

Hair: She _____ hair.

Eyes: She _____ eyes.

Age: She _____ in

    her _____.

Weight: She _____.

C   🔁 Tell a partner about the woman in **B**.

UNIT 2 BEHAVIOR

LESSON A

Review of the Present Continuous Tense			
Affirmative and negative statements			
I	am		
He / She / It	is	(not)	going.
You / We / They	are		

Contractions
I am → I'm
she is → she's
they are → they're

Spelling Rules
work → working
smile → smiling
sit → sitting

Yes / No questions			Short answers	
Is	she		Yes, she is.	No, she's not.* / No, she isn't.
Are	you	smiling?	Yes, I am.	No, I'm not.
	they		Yes, they are.	No, they're not.* / No, they aren't.

*In spoken English, this negative form is more common.

Wh- questions				Answers
Where	are	you	sitting?	(I'm sitting) in the front row.
	is	he		(He's sitting) over there.

A Use the words in parentheses to make questions and statements in the present continuous. Use the correct punctuation.

1. A: _____ (the dog / bark)

   B: I think he's hungry.

2. A: _____ (you / do)

   B: _____ (watch / TV)

3. A: _____ (you / study)

   B: No, I'm not. _____ (I / take a break)

4. A: Where are Eric and Susan?

   B: _____ (come / not / today)

5. A: _____ (it / go)

   B: Not bad. How about you?

6. A: Where's Tina? _____ (she / work)

   B: Yes, she is. She finishes at 5:00.

7. A: _____ (we / win / the game)

   B: _____ (we / no)

LESSON B

Object Pronouns			
Subject	**Verb**	**Object**	In English, an object pronoun (*them*) can replace a noun (*my parents*).
Leo	knows	my parents. **them**.	

I love my parents. My parents love **me**.

You need help. I can help **you**.*

He / She knows Jon. Jon knows **him / her**.

It is expensive. I can't buy **it**.

We are having a party. Please join **us**.

They are popular. Everyone likes **them**.

Subject pronouns come before a verb:

I *love* my parents.

Object pronouns come after...

a verb: My parents *love* me.

a preposition: Jon is angry *at* **her**.

*For both singular and plural *you*

A Complete the sentences with the correct subject and object pronouns.

1. <u>David</u> kisses <u>his mother</u> every day.
   subject   object

   _____He_____ kisses _____her_____ every day.

2. <u>Mrs. Wang</u> is shouting at <u>Carlos</u>.

   _____ is shouting at _____.

3. <u>The dog</u> is barking at <u>Simone and me</u>.

   _____ is barking at _____.

4. <u>Simone and I</u> are nervous about <u>the test</u>.

   _____ are nervous about _____.

5. In Japan, <u>people</u> give <u>business cards</u> with two hands.

   In Japan, _____ give _____ with two hands.

6. <u>I</u> am waving to <u>you and Leo</u>.

   I am waving to _____. Can you see _____?

B Read the sentences. Underline the subject. Circle the object.

1. <u>Angie</u> is waving to (her son).

2. Tom is smiling at Jane.

3. Carlos is worried about the test.

4. Do your parents like Indian food?

5. Peter and Cindy are talking to Bill and Anna.

6. Rick and I can meet you and Mike at 3:00.

7. The dog is barking at Taylor and me.

8. Maya is calling David on her cell phone.

C Rewrite the sentences in **B**. Use the correct subject and object pronouns.

1. *She's waving to him* _____.

2. _____.

3. _____.

4. _____.

5. _____.

6. _____.

7. _____.

8. _____.

UNIT **3** HEROES

LESSON A

Past Forms of *be*
am / is → **was**
am not / isn't → **wasn't**
are → **were**
aren't → **weren't**

The Simple Past Tense with *be*

Affirmative and Negative Statements		
Subject	***was / were***	
I	**was** / **wasn't**	
You	**were** / **weren't**	brave.
He / She / It	**was** / **wasn't**	
We / You / They	**were** / **weren't**	

Yes / No Questions			Answers
Was / Were	**Subject**		
Were	you	brave?	Yes, I **was**. / No, I **wasn't**.
	they		Yes, they **were**. / No, they **weren't**.
Was	she		Yes, she **was**. / No, she **wasn't**.
	I		Yes, you **were**. / No, you **weren't**.

Wh- Questions				Answers
***Wh-* word**	***was / were***	**Subject**		
Where	**were**	you	yesterday?	At home.
When	**was**	he	in Iceland?	Two years ago.
Who	**was**	your teacher	last semester?	Ms. Hunter.

You can use these time expressions with the past tense of *be*: *yesterday,* **in** *1990,* **last** *semester / week, two days / years* **ago**.

A Complete the conversation with a partner. Use the correct form of the verb *be* in the past tense.

TIM: Hi, Kelly. It's Tim. I called you yesterday, but you (1. not) _____ home.

KELLY: I (2.) _____ at the library. I'm writing a paper about Pierre and Marie Curie.

TIM: They (3.) _____ scientists from France, right?

KELLY: Right. Well, actually Pierre (4.) _____ French, but his wife (5. not) _____ born in France. She (6.) _____ from Poland. She (7.) _____ also the first person to win a Nobel Prize twice.

B Complete the questions on the left. Then match them with the correct answers on the right.

1. _____ Kelly at home?
2. _____ _____ Kelly?
3. _____ the Curies scientists?
4. _____ Marie Curie born in France?
5. _____ _____ Marie Curie born?
6. _____ Marie Curie the first person to win two Nobel Prizes?
7. _____ _____ Pierre Curie from?
8. _____ _____ the Curies?

a. Yes, they were.
b. No, she wasn't.
c. No, she wasn't.
d. They were scientists.
e. Yes, she was.
f. France.
g. At the library.
h. In Poland.

LESSON B

The Simple Past: Affirmative and Negative Statements		
I / You / He / She / We / They	visit**ed** **didn't** visit	Tokyo.
I / You / He / She / We / They	start**ed** **didn't** start	a company.

In the simple past tense, the verb form is the same for all persons.

In affirmative statements, add *–ed* or *–d*. See the spelling rules below.

In negative statements, use *did not* or *didn't* + the base form of the verb.

The Simple Past Tense of Regular Verbs: Spelling Rules	
move → mov**ed**	If the verb ends in *e*, add *–d*.
start → start**ed**	If the verb ends with a consonant, add *–ed*.
stu**dy** → stud**ied**	If the verb ends with a consonant + *y*, change the *y* to *i* and add *–ed*.
pla**y** → play**ed**	If the verb ends with a vowel + *y*, add *–ed*.
stop → stop**ped**	With one-syllable verbs that end with a consonant–vowel–consonant, double the last letter and add *–ed*.
fi**x** → fix**ed**	But do not double the last consonant if it is a *w* or *x*.
oc**cur** → occur**red**	With two-syllable verbs that end with a consonant–vowel–consonant, double the last consonant if the last syllable is stressed.
lis**ten** → listen**ed**	But do not double the last consonant if the last syllable is not stressed.

A Complete the sentences with the simple past tense of each verb. Pay attention to spelling.

1. Sanga Moses (work) _____ in a bank in the capital.

2. One day, he (visit) _____ his family.

3. He saw his sister. She (carry) _____ a lot of wood that day.

4. She (look) _____ at her brother, and she (cry) _____. She said,
   "I (not go) _____ to school today. I (walk) _____ 10 kilometers to get wood."

5. Sanga Moses (want) _____ his sister to stay in school.

6. That day, he (decide) _____ to do something. He (stop) _____ working at the bank.
   He (start) _____ Eco-Fuel Africa.

7. With a group of engineers, he (invent) _____ a new oven. It (change) _____ many
   people's lives in Uganda.

B Make sentences about things you did or didn't do yesterday. Use the verbs.

1. walk to school _____ I didn't walk to school. _____
2. text a friend _____
3. listen to a song in English _____
4. study for a test _____
5. cook dinner _____
6. watch TV _____
7. hug my mom _____
8. wash my hair _____

UNIT **4** AT THE MOVIES

LESSON A

The Present Continuous as Future			
Subject + *be*	**Verb + *ing***		**Future time expression**
We're	seeing	a movie	today / tonight / tomorrow.
			in an hour.
			this weekend.
They're	making		next year.

You can use the present continuous tense (often with a future time expression) to talk about future plans.

Use the present continuous only when a plan exists:

Here's the plan: We're meeting downtown and then driving to the theater in my car.

Do not use the present continuous to make predictions. Use *going to* instead:

~~*He's passing the test tomorrow.*~~ *He's going to pass the test tomorrow.*

A Complete the conversation. Use the present continuous form of the verbs in parentheses and complete the time expression with the words in the box.

> Verbs that are related to movement and travel (like *go, come, take, fly, travel, visit, leave, arrive,* and *get*) are commonly used in the present continuous when expressing future time.

| in | next | this | tomorrow |

A: I'm really looking forward to summer vacation (1.) ___this___ year.

B: Why is that?

A: Because (2. I / go) _____ to Tanzania, in Africa. (3. we / leave) _____ (4.) _____ morning! I'm so excited!

B: Wow! How (5. you / get) _____ there?

A: (6. we / fly) _____ with Global Airways from New York City. And (7. we / change) _____ planes in Dubai before arriving in Dar es Salaam.

B: Do you already have a plan for the trip?

A: Yes, (8. we / visit) _____ Zanzibar for a few days and then (9. climb) _____ Mount Kilimanjaro.

B: Great! How long is the trip?

A: (10. I / stay) _____ for two weeks, so (11. I / return) _____ early (12.) _____ month. (13. my friend / travel) _____ an extra week in Africa. What about you? (14. you / go) _____ anywhere fun?

B: Not really. (15. I / visit) _____ my family down south. (16. I / drive) _____ and (17. I / leave) _____ (18.) _____ a few hours.

LESSON B

-*ed* Adjectives	-*ing* Adjectives
1a. I'm **bored**. I don't like this movie.	**1b.** This movie is **boring**. Let's watch something else.
2a. I was **surprised** by the ending.	**2b.** The end of the movie was **surprising**.

Use -*ed* adjectives to describe a person's feelings. For example, in sentence 1a, you can say *I'm bored*, (meaning "I feel bored") but not ~~I'm boring~~.

Use -*ing* adjectives to describe a situation, an activity, or person that makes you feel a certain way: *That movie was boring. My math teacher is very inspiring.*

Here are some common -*ed* / -*ing* adjectives. Review their meanings with your instructor and classmates.

amazed / amazing	embarrassed / embarrassing	interested / interesting
bored / boring	entertained / entertaining	relaxed / relaxing
confused / confusing	excited / exciting	shocked / shocking
depressed / depressing	frightened / frightening	surprised / surprising
disappointed / disappointing	inspired / inspiring	terrified / terrifying

A Complete the movie review. Circle the correct words. Did Paula like the movie?

Actor Sean Clarkson is in the new sci-fi thriller *Midnight on the Moon*. Overall, I was very disappointed / disappointing with this film. Some scenes in the film are excited / exciting, and newcomer Kristin Cox is interested / interesting as Clarkson's love interest in the movie. But the story is often confused / confusing. I didn't understand the ending at all. I was also surprised / surprising by some scenes in the film. They were very violent!

B Complete the sentences with the correct form of the words in the box.

bore	confuse	depress	embarrass	entertain	surprise	terrify

1. I was kind of _____ after watching that movie. It was a tearjerker!

2. I'm _____. Is our test this Friday or next Friday?

3. My film class is very _____. It's a lot of fun.

4. I watched a scary movie alone, and I was _____. It was very frightening!

5. When that movie won Best Film, it was _____. In my opinion, it was a terrible movie.

6. This movie is very _____—not interesting at all.

7. I fell asleep during class, and the teacher yelled at me. How _____!

ADDITIONAL GRAMMAR NOTES

Possessive Nouns		
Singular nouns (+ 's)	**Plural nouns (+ ')**	**Irregular plural nouns (+ 's)**
sister → sister**'s**	parents → parent**s'**	children → children**'s**
brother → brother**'s**	brothers → brother**s'**	women → women**'s**
For first and last names that end in *s*, you can add **'s** or just **'**.		

A Look up the word *twin* in a dictionary. Read about Hallie Parker and Annie James from the movie *The Parent Trap.* Complete the sentences with a singular noun, a plural noun, or a possessive noun.

1. Hallie Parker lives in her (father) _____ home in California, in the US.

2. Annie (James) _____ home is in London. She lives there with her (mother) _____.

3. The two (girl) _____, Hallie and Annie, are (twin) _____! But they live apart. They don't know about each other.

4. (Hallie) _____ summer plans are exciting. She's going to summer camp. And by chance, (Annie) _____ is going to the same summer camp!

5. At camp, Hallie sees her (sister) _____ face for the first time. They look the same! They are both surprised and happy.

6. Hallie doesn't know her (mom) _____ name, and Annie doesn't know her (dad) _____ name.

7. Before the two (child) _____ leave camp, they have an idea. The two (sister) _____ plan is an exciting one!

B 🔁 What do you think happens next? Write three sentences. Tell your partner.

_____.

_____.

_____.

	Possessive Adjectives	Possessive Pronouns	*belong to*
Whose passport is this?	It's **my** passport.	It's **mine**.	It **belongs to me**.
	your	**yours**.	**you**.
	her	**hers**.	**her**.
	his	**his**.	**him**.
	our	**ours**.	**us**.
	their	**theirs**.	**them**.

Whose and *who's* have the same pronunciation but different meanings.
Whose asks about the owner of something: *Whose house is that? It's mine.*
Who's is a contraction of *Who* and *is*: *Who's studying English? Maria is.*

A Write the correct possessive pronoun for the underlined words.

1. A: That's not her suitcase.

   B: No, <u>her suitcase</u> is over there.

2. A: Can I use your cell phone? <u>My cell phone</u> doesn't work.

   B: Sorry, but I forgot my cell phone at home. Use <u>Jon's phone</u>.

3. A: Is your class fun?

   B: Yes, but <u>Aya and Leo's class</u> is more interesting.

4. A: Is your hometown hot in the summer? <u>My hometown</u> is.

   B: <u>Our hometown</u> is, too.

5. A: Your birthday is in May.

   B: That's right, and <u>your birthday</u> is in March.

B 🔁 Use the words in the chart to complete the conversation. Then practice the dialog with a partner.

JIM: Well, I have (1.) ___my___ luggage. Where's
(2.) _____ ?

BEN: Um... let's see... oh, here's (3.) _____
suitcase. No, wait... this one isn't (4.) _____ .

JIM: (5.) _____ is it?

BEN: It says Mr. Simon Konig. It belongs to
(6.) _____ .

JIM: Hey, I think that man has (7.) _____
suitcase. See? He probably thinks it's
(8.) _____ .

BEN: I'll ask him. Excuse me, does this suitcase
belong to (9.) _____ ?

SIMON: Oh, sorry. My mistake! I thought it was (10.) _____ !

The Simple Past: Affirmative and Negative Statements (Irregular Verbs)

Subject	*did + not*	Verb	
I / You / He / She / We / They		forgot	her birthday.
	didn't	forget	

- In affirmative statements, do not add *-ed* to form irregular past tense verbs. See the chart below for the simple past tense form of many common irregular verbs.
- In negative statements, use *did not* or *didn't* + the base form of the verb.

Present	Past	Present	Past	Present	Past	Present	Past	Present	Past
begin	began	drink	drank	give	gave	meet	met	sing	sang
bring	brought	eat	ate	go	went	pay	paid	speak	spoke
buy	bought	fall	fell	have	had	read	read*	take	took
choose	chose	feel	felt	know	knew	run	ran	teach	taught
come	came	forget	forgot	leave	left	say	said	think	thought
do	did	get	got	make	made	see	saw	wear	wore

*Note: There is a vowel shift in the past tense pronunciation of *read*. The vowel goes from /i/ to /ɛ/.

A Complete the story with the simple past form of the verbs in parentheses. Most of the verbs are irregular. Which ones are regular?

A Scary Memory

There (1. be) _____ a fire one day when I (2. be) _____ at school. It (3. begin) _____ around lunchtime. Soon, we all (4. smell) _____ smoke. Someone (5. say) _____ in a loud voice, "Fire!" Then the fire alarm (6. ring) _____. As we (7. walk) _____ down the hallway, I (8. feel) _____ the heat from the fire. We (9. not say) _____ anything—everyone was so quiet.

The fire truck (10. come) _____ quickly. The firefighters (11. run) _____ into the building and (12. stop) _____ the fire. After 30 minutes, we (13. go) _____ back into our school. Luckily, there (14. not be) _____ much damage. I will never forget that day.

B 🔁 Take turns reading the story in **A** with a partner. Then explain the story in your own words. Can you retell it from memory?

The Simple Past Tense: *Yes / No* Questions

Did	Subject	Verb		Short answers
Did	you he / she / it they	stay up late wake up	last night?	Yes, I did. / No, I didn't. Yes, he did. / No, he didn't. Yes, they did. / No, they didn't.

- To ask a past tense *Yes / No* question, use *did* + subject + base form of the verb.
- Short answers are the same for both regular and irregular verbs.

The Simple Past Tense: *Wh-* Questions

Wh- word	did	Subject	Verb	Answers
When	did	you he / she / it they	study?	(I / She / They studied) last night.
			get up?	(I / She / They got up) at 7:00.
What			happened to you?	I woke up late this morning.

A Circle the mistake in each dialog and correct it.

1. A: Did Mario stayed up late last night?

   B: Yes, he did.

2. A: Did you forget your keys?

   B: No, I didn't forgot them.

3. A: Where did Julie went on her vacation?

   B: She went to Mexico.

4. A: What did happen to Yu and Amy?

   B: They slept late and missed the bus.

B Complete the dialogs with a past tense *Yes / No* or *Wh-* question or short answer.

1. A: _____ last night?

   B: I went to bed at 10:00.

2. A: _____ well?

   B: No, I didn't sleep well. I had nightmares.

3. A: _____ before bed?

   B: No, _____. I never drink coffee before bed.

4. A: Did you eat before bed?

   B: Yes, _____.

5. A: _____ last night?

   B: I ate a piece of cake. Maybe that caused the bad dreams.

6. A: _____ about?

   B: I dreamt about zombies.

C Practice the conversations in **B** with a partner.

The Future with *be going to*

Subject	be	(not)	*going to*	Base form		Future time expression
I	**am**					tomorrow.
You	**are**					this fall.
He / She	**is**	(not)	**going to**	start	college	in August.
We / You / They	**are**					next week / month / year.
						after graduation.

Use *be going to* to talk about future plans.

You can also use it to make predictions: *She's going to be a great doctor.*

When the subject is a pronoun, it's common to use a contraction with *be*: *I'm going to start college...*

With a noun + *be going to*, we often say the contraction: *My sister's going to take some time off.*

Don't use the contraction in formal writing.

	Yes / No questions					Short answers	
Is	she					Yes, she is.	No, she's not. / No, she isn't.
Are	you	**going to**	start	college	this fall?	Yes, I am.	No, I'm not.
	they					Yes, they are.	No, they're not. / No they aren't.

		Wh- questions				Answers
When	is	he	**going to**	start	college?	(He's / I'm going to start college) in August.
	are	you				

A Complete the sentences about a student's summer plans with the correct form of *be going to*.

I (1. visit) _____ Europe after graduation. My brother (2. stay) _____

home. He (3. not travel) _____ anywhere. He (4. take) _____ it easy.

My parents (5. take) _____ a week off from work. They (6. meet) _____

me in Paris. We (7. not return) _____ home until September 5.

B Complete the conversation using questions and answers with *be going to*.

JO: So, (1. when / you / leave) _____ for Europe?

NEIL: Next month.

JO: (2. you / go) _____ alone?

NEIL: No, (3. my roommate / come) _____ with me.

JO: (4. Where / you / start) _____ your trip?

NEIL: First, (5. we / fly) _____ to London.
Then (6. I / visit) _____ two more cities alone.

JO: (7. your / parents / visit) _____ you in Europe?

NEIL: Yes, (8. they / meet) _____ me in Paris.

C 🔁 In your notebook, write three *be going to* questions to ask about your partner's summer plans. Then interview your partner.

NOTES